Praise for Corinne Hofmann

'It is the most extraordinary story (as the four million people who have already bought the book in Europe would no doubt agree!)' – Robert Gwyn Palmer, *Sunday Telegraph*

'What an amazing story! One of the bravest and most vivid I've read in years, I'm not surprised it's a bestseller' – Deborah Moggach

'Hofmann is a brilliant observer … a talented writer, describing with unflinching detail the consequences of a passion that combines the element of a holiday romance with troubling fantasies about the noble savage. Gripping' – Joan Smith, *Independent*

'It's an astonishing story of love at first sight. So astonishing, it would become a bestselling book and a hit movie, fascinating readers and audiences around the world. She was white, well-educated, from wealthy Switzerland. He was a Masai warrior from a remote village in the poorest part of Kenya. They didn't speak the same language, they knew nothing about each other, yet, from the first glance, they just clicked. It sounds like a Mills & Boon romance, doesn't it, except every word of it is true, even down to the white wedding and a beautiful baby daughter. But now there's a new twist – the surprising final chapter of *The White Masai* …' – *60 Minutes*

'It shows the strength of love at first sight' – Desmond Morris

'Just try to put this down' – *People*

'A startling experience with riveting exotica and intriguing human relationships' – *Hollywood Reporter*

'An affecting richness … Seekers of romance and adventure will be amply rewarded' – *Publishers Weekly* (starred review)

'The hit book *The White Masai* … an extraordinary story' – Libby Purves, BBC *Midweek*

'A deliciously readable book – it really is possible to gulp it down in one long sitting. *The White Masai* has already sold four million copies and has been turned into a Hollywood film … Corinne Hofmann has struck gold' – Kathryn Hughes, *Mail on Sunday*

'At once a captivating romance and a breathtaking travelogue into the Kenyan outback, *The White Masai* carries us on an epic journey. Based on the autobiography of Corinne Hofmann, one of the most popular books in Europe of the past decade, it tells the unbelievable – yet true – fish-out-of-water tale of a white European woman who becomes the wife of a Masai warrior. The exotic urban jungle of Mombasa – where the two first fall in love – and the tiny village surrounded by majestic landscapes where they make their home provide a backdrop that is nothing short of extraordinary' – *Femail*

'A fascinating film, a culture clash of intimate proportions. The view of Samburu life is amazing' – ABC

'The film is beautifully shot, engrossing, with realistic performances and some genuine moments of charm and horror. A scene in which Carola tries to help a woman who is miscarrying, and Lemalian will not assist because the woman is bewitched, will strike terror in most viewer's hearts' – *Sydney Morning Herald*

'An extraordinary and unputdownable tale' – *Bookseller*

'*The White Masai* has already sold four million copies in Europe and has now been turned into a big Hollywood film. These successes suggest that, in publishing terms at least, Corinne Hofmann has finally struck gold' – *Ireland on Sunday*

'An extraordinary and unputdownable tale' – *Bookseller*

'It's a truly riveting read, better than any reality TV show' – *Publishing News*

'A dashing tale of love and adventure in contemporary Kenya. Corinne is bewitched by the exotic beauty of a man who lives in a hut in the back of beyond. There are some wonderfully loving and sensual moments … what a story' – Mavis Cheek, Critic's Choice, *Daily Mail*

Africa, My Passion

AFRICA, MY PASSION

CORINNE HOFMANN

Translated from the German by Peter Millar

ARCADIA BOOKS

Arcadia Books Ltd
139 Highlever Road
London W10 6PH

www.arcadiabooks.co.uk

First published in the UK by Arcadia Books 2014

Originally published by A1 Verlag GmbH, München, as
Afrika, meine Passion, 2011
Copyright © A1 Verlag GmbH, München 2011

This English translation from the German
Copyright © Peter Millar 2014

Picture credits:
Plates 1/2/3/4/5/6 © Corinne Hofmann/A1 Verlag
Plates 7/8/9/10 © Klaus Kamphausen/A1 Verlag
Plate 11 © Privat/A1 Verlag
Plates 12/13/14/15/16 © Klaus Kamphausen/Albert Völkmann/A1 Verlag

A catalogue record for this book is available from the British Library.

ISBN 978-1-90812-945-1

Typeset in Minion by MacGuru Ltd
Printed and bound by CPI Group (UK) Ltd., Croydon CRO 4YY

Arcadia Books supports English PEN *www.englishpen.org* and
The Book Trade Charity *http://booktradecharity.wordpress.com*

Arcadia Books distributors are as follows:

in the UK and elsewhere in Europe:
Macmillan Distribution Ltd
Brunel Road
Houndmills
Basingstoke
Hants RG21 6XS

in the USA and Canada:
Dufour Editions
PO Box 7
Chester Springs
PA 19425

in Australia/New Zealand:
NewSouth Books
c/o TL Distribution
15–23 Helles Avenue Moorebank
NSW 2170

CONTENTS

FAREWELL TO THE WHITE MASAI, BUT IT'S STILL BACK TO AFRICA

Ten years of being the White Masai was enough, I thought. On 25 October 2008 I did my final book reading in front of an enthusiastic audience in the little town of Lauchhammer in Brandenburg, north-east Germany. When the audience applauded, my emotions were mixed: I left the stage to applause but with a tear as well as a smile in my eye as I sat down at the little table to do my very last book signing. Many of those present came up to me, shook my hand and said, 'Frau Hoffmann, you have to keep on writing. You have such a fascinating life. How are your African family getting on, and when will your daughter get to meet her father again?' Throughout the hour I was signing books, I was told time and again that my writing had touched the hearts of the audience and made a country they knew little about fascinating.

I really did enjoy all those book readings but it had reached a point where I thought I had to put Africa and the White Masai behind me. Two weeks later I set off with a female friend on a four-week trip around India, a country that had always fascinated me. Four weeks obviously isn't very much time to get to experience an entirely different culture, but it was a start. We decided to concentrate on northern India.

Our first stop is the huge metropolis of Delhi, a city where we feel swamped by the sheer mass of people. We hire a car and a driver to get us safely between the swarms of rickshaws and bicycle taxis as we move from one sight to another. It's fascinating but I realise that travelling like this means we have little contact with ordinary people.

As we pass a market I ask the driver to stop so I can get out and explore on foot. Before I can really get to know a country, I need to drink in the smells, tastes and feel of it, experience it for myself, rather than seeing it all through the dusty windows of a cab. The driver isn't keen. 'Even as an Indian I wouldn't get out and walk around here.' Nonetheless, we get out and all of a sudden I feel better even though there are hundreds of people staring at us.

One man has lots of large fish laid out on the ground underneath a little table, on which a huge variety of seafood is laid out for sale, while he himself squats on the table next to it all. The crabs, mussels and little fish are lying there right next to his naked feet, while hordes of people walk past only a few inches away. A little further on a man in a white apron is cooking something in various pots, while men sit on the road in front of him waiting to be fed. People with heavily laden handcarts constantly push past us, while beggars hold out their hands to us. Smells of every description fill the air, from spicy cooked food to brackish dirty water, and everywhere the smell of fish.

We spot one butcher with hacked-up hunks of meat in heaps in front of him. There are three bloody heads of animals with blue-painted horns lying on a sheet of plastic, their severed hooves next to them, while behind them another plastic sheet, red this time, serves as a display counter for the rest of the meat. The stench of blood fills the air. The butcher hacks at the rest of the corpse with an axe, while his young son, who looks about nine, helps him. We find ourselves treading in guts and entrails lying all over the ground.

It may not exactly be what we would call hygienic, but there is no doubt that it reeks of life. My heart leaps with memories of 'my' Africa; this reminds me of Nairobi.

During the rest of our trip we visit wonderful palaces, museums and lots of other sights, including a wedding that feels like something out of a fairy tale from the *The Arabian Tales*. I enjoy it all, but the constant feeling nags at me that I am seeing it through the eyes of a tourist.

Things change however when we travel towards Pushkar, a beautiful little town on the edge of the Thar Desert with the little holy Lake Pushkar at its heart. On the way there I notice changes in the landscape as it becomes more arid. I see women wandering along in bright red or pink saris and it all reminds me of Barsaloi, my home in Kenya for all those years. The colours and the wild landscape trigger a longing deep within me. It is incredible how strongly my past calls out to me. And the call becomes stronger with every kilometre. I begin to see parallels with the Samburu country everywhere, particularly the sight of women struggling to fill jugs or canisters with water and then carry them home on their heads. It is as if I am right back home.

It is crazy. Coming to India was meant to release me from the pull I feel towards Africa, but it makes me feel as if I am right back in Kenya. I know that I am starting to get on my friend's nerves. 'Corinne, we're in India, not Africa,' she says tetchily.

'I know,' I reply. 'But there's something pulling on my heartstrings. Up until now I've been amazed by the things we've seen, but none of them has moved me like this.'

Our next destination, an hour's flying time from Pushkar, is Mumbai. It comes as a bit of culture shock to see the women and girls here dressed so fashionably and behaving so normally. Welcome to the modern world! Getting about this overpopulated megacity is exciting but very stressful, and we decide to reward ourselves with a four-day break at a magnificent beach resort in southern India.

On the way to the hotel we are astonished to see so many heavily armed police outside the building. Every car is being thoroughly searched. Both we and our luggage have to be scanned. We can only assume some VIP is staying in the building. It's only later that we find out from the television about the terrible terrorist attack that hit Mumbai just after we left, with hostages taken and numerous fatalities. Several people were even killed in one of the bars we had used. We watch the news reports in horror with our hearts racing, thanking God that we are still alive. My guardian angel watched over me again.

In late November I return to my home in Lugano, Switzerland. India fascinated me but didn't move me like Africa. Perhaps I should have stayed longer and taken more time at each destination. But I think it is just that Africa is unique. The minute you step off the plane you can feel the vibrations in the air. Just travelling around you are embraced by pulsating energy and by the warmth of the people. That was something I didn't encounter in India.

December arrives with a chill. While everybody is getting ready for Christmas, I have to make a mental adjustment: there was no run-up to Christmas in India.

For me, as no doubt for many, the year's end brings poignant thoughts to mind, of what has happened over the last twelve months and what the new year may bring. Unfortunately the India trip didn't give me any fresh ideas about what to do with my life, but then, I am lucky enough that I don't need to worry about money. I can take my time.

On the evening of 30 December I'm lying in bed flicking

through a travel magazine with a superb picture of India on the cover, when suddenly I spot an advert that immediately grabs my attention: 'Where the world is still wild: Nature photographer and adventurer seeks author or travel companion for expeditions; currently setting off on a camel trek. Any interest?'

Any interest! One of my great loves is mountain walking. I lie awake much of the night wondering what might lie behind the ad. What does the person who put it in mean by 'wild' and 'adventurer'? My own experiences in the African bush mean I'm not easily impressed. But next morning my mind is made up. Corinne, I tell myself, write to this man and you're bound to get some sort of interesting reaction. It's got to be a good way to start the new year.

So, on the very last day of the old year, I send an email to the advertiser expressing my interest and within two hours I have an answer. It turns out that he is planning a six-week desert trek through northern Namibia. Africa again! My heart leaps. Even before I head out for a New Year's Eve party in Zurich, I'm bursting with enthusiasm for a new adventure.

Namibia borders South Africa to the south and Angola to the north, with the Kunene as the northern border where, in the so-called Kaoko Veldt, the Himba tribe lives. They happen to be a tribe that has fascinated me for a long time. Along with the Samburu and the Masai they are among the last semi-nomadic tribes in Africa. For ages I've had two large photographs of beautiful Himba women hanging in my flat. They immediately grab the attention with their skin painted red, their hair dyed red and woven into tight braids.

A week later I finally meet up with my 'adventurer'. I get on well with him, even if at times he seems a bit domineering, but his outline of the planned trip seems to be well thought out. We will trek through the veldt, led by a local camel herder who will supply us with a couple of camels to carry our bags. Travelling like this will give us lots of opportunity to make contact with the Himba, not least because they are unfamiliar with camels in the north. We talk over the details and I make my mind up that the trip is for me. Six weeks trekking, cooking on a campfire, sleeping in the open, making our way across the veldt and watching the wild animals – just what I'm looking for. Obviously there could be personal problems. I will be committing myself to travelling with two men I've never met before in a wilderness with no mobile phone reception.

But I've never been timid, and I can always take a satellite phone in case of emergencies. Ten days later I let the adventurer know that I will be coming along, not as an author but as a travelling companion.

Obviously a lot of my friends and relatives are keen to tell me I've been a bit premature in making up my mind so quickly. But that's just the way I am. When I go for something, I go for it straight away. Apart from anything else this is the first time in years I haven't had anything else on my plate. There are no book readings to turn up for, no contracts to adhere to. My daughter has finished her make-up course and is now studying hairdressing with the aim of getting into the cinema, television or fashion world.

I tell myself that walking for days on end across a desert, far from civilisation, in the company of a couple of good-natured docile camels will give me a new perspective on life. A long walk is like meditation: good for the soul.

THE HARD SLOG THROUGH
THE HIMBA HOMELAND

We finally set off on 15 May 2009. I fly to Windhoek, although even that does not go as smoothly as planned. Just three hours before departure the Swiss airline flight is cancelled and they tell me to come back the next day. That's no good, because I am booked on a ten-day warm-up programme that starts tomorrow. Over the ten days, we are going to visit the famed Etosha National Park and then take a six-day trek along the Kunene River. Four others, including my two companions on the expedition, are also going on the trek and it seemed sensible to join them to get acclimatised and get to know the pair better before setting off with them on my own. I therefore really have to get on a flight today.

After a flurry of telephone calls I dash up to Frankfurt and manage to catch a flight with Lufthansa. Four hours later we're flying over Kenya and my heart is thumping. It has been six years since I last saw my family there. But I have made up my mind that I'm only going to go back when my daughter is interested enough to discover her African roots. How on earth could I ever explain to her father and her dear old grandmother why I had turned up again on my own? In just a year's time I will indeed be back there, not least because of the influence of this Namibian trip.

We land at Windhoek but after waiting for what seems for ever, I have to accept that my luggage didn't come with me.

Hardly an auspicious beginning, setting out on a trek without any of the stuff I brought with me. At least I'm wearing my sturdy walking shoes and have packed my expensive sleeping bag in my hand baggage. But it's hardly an ideal situation as we're setting off first thing in the morning on a journey of several hundred kilometres. And I'm going to need rather more than the clothes on my back over the next two months. Nonetheless, there's no alternative but to climb into the waiting minibus and drive off.

Windhoek is completely different to the cities I know in East Africa. Lots of the streets, bakeries, bookshops and other businesses still have German names. And there aren't the hordes of people I'm used to seeing bustling along the streets. No sooner have we left the city, however, than the minibus comes to a spluttering halt at the side of the road. The accelerator pedal has broken. To make matters worse, it's Sunday. I'm beginning to think this trip is doomed. First the flight is cancelled, then my luggage goes astray and now there's problem number three. What else can possibly go wrong?

The expedition leader makes a few phone calls and eventually the minibus gets towed to a garage where a couple of mechanics in their Sunday best crawl under the car and weld the accelerator back on. At last we're off again.

We head north along a well-made tarmac road that runs straight as a ruler. There are fences on either side of the highway as far as the eye can see. A few kilometres further on the style and colour of the fencing changes, indicating that we're travelling over somebody else's land. I learn that the land is mostly owned by cattle farmers who make the most of their vast land-holdings by running safaris on the side.

We hardly see another human being apart from those in passing cars. Namibia is very thinly populated, with a total of barely two million inhabitants, in a country twice the size of Germany. It's several hours before we come across the first pedestrians, and shortly after that we come into a small village.

It's been pouring with rain over the past few days and there's substantial flooding.

Eventually we reach the famed Etosha National Park. We're due to spend two nights here so we'll already be under canvas. The Etosha Plain was once a lake that evaporated. Normally it is white with the residual salt, but right now it looks like a lake again. A calm sea of water stretches all the way to the distant horizon. As we drive along the edge of it we come across lots of giraffes and now and then we have to stop for a panicky ostrich or two. We also find ourselves gawping at distant zebras, impalas, wild pigs and all sorts of bird life. It is fabulous staring across this shimmering deep-blue and occasionally silver sea. The wild savannah grasses and sparse bushes contrast vividly with the cloudless blue sky. I could look at it all for ever.

There's a watering hole not far from where we are to pitch tent for the night, allowing us to get a closer view of the animals. We are lucky to find a large herd of zebras and gnus heading for the water. There are so many of them that they jostle one another to get at the drinking water, though the zebras keep looking round to make sure there are no signs of lions approaching. But there are only a few jackals that send birds flapping into the air and none of the other animals seem much worried by them.

At night the watering hole is lit up for us to give us a better view, which is amazing because we observe a herd of elephants trotting up to the water, making slurping noises as they use their trunks to take the water to their mouths. Before long two rhinos come and join them. It is mesmerising. We are just sitting there, on the other side on an electrified fence, watching this spectacle as though it were a live show laid on for us.

Later I lie there in my tent listening to the noise of the wild world outside. Some animal – I have no idea what – comes up and snuffles against the tent wall. At one stage the roar of a lion from the watering hole wakes me up. It would appear one of the other animals has been taken by it. I'm tempted to get up and run to the observation area, but it's too cold and dark, so instead I just lie there with my pulse racing.

The next day we set off again through the vast national park and find ourselves continually amazed by the wonder of nature on display. It's all magnificent but deep down I can't wait to get started on the trek and see the real wilderness beyond the fence.

About a thousand kilometres on we come to the Okangwati District where the trek officially starts. It looks great, very dry and savannah-like, and reminds me a lot of the Maralal area in Kenya. There are no more fences here.

We set up our tents on land owned by a couple of expat Germans working for a local charity where the lady of the house entertains us. Around nine o' clock a car drives up in the darkness and a man climbs out with my big, heavy suitcase in his hand. I can hardly believe that after all my phone calls and pleading, my suitcase has finally arrived just in time. The man who's brought it has driven a thousand kilometres and has to head back again to Windhoek tonight. I'm immensely grateful for his dedication to bringing my belongings to me, and I'm delighted to get a change of clothes for the first time in days.

I meet my first Himba just after breakfast: two elderly ladies crossing the dried-up riverbed to get to the centre of the village, a collection of a few bars, three basic shops and, of course, several churches. Both women are covered from head to toe, including their hair, with red ghee. Looking at the Himba, you would hardly use the term 'black African' to describe them.

The red fat protects their skin from both the heat and the cold and also protects them against mosquitoes. It's as if it were an extra item of clothing. Both old ladies are carrying huge loads on their heads, packed in bags made of cloth or goat leather, also coloured red. Their long, carefully braided hair hangs down, and between their naked breasts they wear a white snail shell as well as pretty necklaces around their necks. I am most impressed by their ochre-red skirts, which are short in front, almost like a mini skirt, but hang down to their calves at the rear. Neither of them have shoes on but, like all Himba, wear heavy silver decorations, about fifteen centimetres long, on their shins.

Despite their age, they move nimbly as they make their way across the sandy dried-up riverbed. This first glimpse of these tribespeople makes me finally feel I'm back in the Africa that I love. Just the sight of them moves me to tears. They remind me too much of the Samburu women back in Barsaloi.

There is still a little time before we set off, so I go for a stroll around the centre of the village. Here I keep bumping into the 'red people', sometimes young girls with budding breasts and huge baskets on their heads making for the market, sometimes mother with babes in arms sitting outside a bar. I'm amazed how much alcohol there is for sale. They don't just drink beer but spirits too. There's disco music blaring from one of the bars, a billiard table in the middle of the main room with three young Himba men playing. It's a bizarre scene: they're wearing modern T-shirts but with thick silver necklaces, their heads shaved on either side but with a great tuft of hair in the middle sticking up wrapped in a cloth or stuffed into a little hat. To my eyes, the females are a lot more attractive than the men. Next to the glowing red females, the men look ridiculous. The women also seem jollier and more inquisitive. They wiggle their bodies naturally to the sound of the music and as I walk along the streets I come across more groups of girls or women standing together chatting and talking while their men stand around grumpily watching them.

After a bit I come to a little market where a Herero woman is selling fragrant herbs. These aren't culinary herbs, but aromatics used as fragrances, leaves or seeds that the young girls use as perfume. Later I discover that some of these herbs are strewn over the embers of a fire and the women squat over them to perfume their more intimate parts. Alongside the sacks of herbs she has some Himba dolls, as well as the red skirts hung on a wooden frame. I feel one of them and am surprised just how heavy it is. It smells of a strange mix of leather, fragrant herbs and rancid butter. I'm not having one of those in my wardrobe.

I'm amazed at how different from the Himba the Herero look, even though the two tribes are closely related, like the Samburu and the Masai. One distinctive difference between the Herero and the Himba is the big hats the Herero women wear at an oblique angle, and their multi-layered ankle-length skirts. The women are clearly proud of their style of dress, even though it was forced on them by missionaries. They are the complete opposite to the scantily clad Himba women.

The far end of the market is what we might call the food hall. Women sit around big open pots in which they cook meat bought from the nearby butcher. There are two half goat carcasses hung up waiting for someone to purchase them.

There's a stark contrast between this traditional idyll and the pickup trucks anomalously parked in front of the clay-walled huts and shops. But everything seems to move at its own pace without any fuss or hustle.

Strolling back to the rest of our group I run across an elderly Himba man heading for one of the bars. Despite his age, he cuts an imposing figure with his height and noble bearing. He is painted red from head to toe and wears a little woolly hat and a pair of aviator sunglasses, and carries a little folding stool in his left hand. He has a machete in a scabbard hanging from his waist, a long stick under his right arm and the usual silver one-piece necklace. He looks at me and says, 'Moro, perivi.' I don't know what it means and just give him an embarrassed smile. Later I'm told it means, 'Hello, how are you?'

Finally, we're off. We climb into the back of the pickup and set off for the rendezvous point where the trek is to start. Tonight we will sleep under canvas in the wilderness for the first time. We each put up our own tents. Suddenly there's a strange growling noise and I look up and see a smiling young man walking towards us leading two camels. This camel herder, who will be with us for the whole six-week expedition, is trying in the gentlest of manners to get the camels to settle down. I'm pleased to see this young Namibian seems to be so good-natured. The camels seem nice too. One look at their thick lips and their big saucer eyes with long eyelashes and you fall in love with them. They are two males, incredibly big and strong. But then they have to be as they're going to be carrying our entire luggage as well as our tents, not to mention food supplies and canisters full of water to last us for six days.

Before long it is night and we sit down to eat around the flickering campfire. Somewhere an animal growls and in the distance a jackal howls. Each of us is sunk in our own thoughts, excited about the journey we are to begin in the morning.

It takes two hours to load up the camels. First of all we have to put blankets over their backs, then an iron frame on to which the luggage and water canisters are fastened. One of the camels seems not too impressed by all this and makes his feeling known loudly. It sounds like a lion roaring, which in the days to come is going to frighten a fair few Himba.

When at last we set off, it's already hot. The expedition leader goes in front with the animals, followed by Lucas, the camel herder. The rest of us follow behind. The pace is brisk, and if I stop to take a photograph I have to run to catch up. We'll be walking for four to five hours a day. I count on my regular hiking in the Swiss Alps to stand me in good stead, but by the second day I'm having problems with the heat and humidity. By noon it's over forty degrees and my clothes are stuck to my body. The rucksack on my back that holds my water bottles and lunch doesn't exactly help.

But the magnificent landscape makes up for the ferocious heat. Most of the time we're walking along a riverbank with bushes, trees and palms on either side. By late afternoon it's time to set up camp for the night. The expedition leader has picked great spots, either under tall trees on the dried up riverbed or right next to the water. Dinner is prepared and we all sit down to eat around the campfire, after which everyone goes to bed early. We're all tired and it's already dark by 5.30 p.m.

Every now and then we run across some Himba or they come to visit our camp. It's always interesting, even if we can't actually talk to them. Sometimes a few lads on donkeys ride up and stare at us; from time to time we spot a Himba woman walking along on her own, presumably off to visit her family.

On the third day we have to cross a river. The water isn't deep but it's very wide. The riverbank is dark and damp and the heavily laden camels are afraid to wade into the river. No matter how we push, pull and shout at them, they refuse to move. They are simply terrified and resist any attempt to get them across. The expedition leader suggests unloading them so they will be lighter and less frightened. Lucas then starts pushing one from behind while the guide pulls him, but the animal stands there, its legs apart, refusing to budge, until eventually it settles down on its knees. If we don't get the camels across the river, that's the end of our trek.

Suddenly a pickup truck appears, a rare occurrence in this isolated area. The driver offers to help and in the end the camel is pulled through the river using his substantial horsepower. In fact, the camel's resistance diminishes markedly when it realises that the wet ground beneath its feet isn't that dangerous. The second camel isn't so hard to move, though its loud bellowing makes perfectly clear what he thinks of it all. Now we have to get all our luggage across and load up the animals again, which takes us another two hours.

It's 3 p.m. by the time we reach our campsite for the night on the other bank. I've got blisters on my feet, which I never get when walking in the mountains. But the extreme heat in the afternoons here makes your feet swell up and soften. I've got blister plasters but in these conditions they don't last long, as they can't stick properly to wet skin. Most of the time we've been walking on dried riverbeds or sandy trails, both of which are hard work. The landscape around us is changing now too: it's starting to get hilly and in the distance we can see small mountain ranges.

One of the most exciting things on the six-day trek was

coming across our first Himba village. From a long way off we can see the corral and hear dogs barking and children shouting. The Himba, just like the Masai, build huts made out of mud and cow dung in a circle, surrounded with a thorn bush fence for protection. A similar fence runs down the middle of the corral, with the cows penned in on one side of it.

It's busy in the village and as we get near, people come out to stare at the camels in amazement. A few small children even burst into tears of terror. The goats start bleating and the dogs start barking.

Two little girls sit on top of a flat-roofed hut filling a basket with dried maize cobs, which an old lady then spreads out on a tarpaulin for other children to remove the kernels. It's easy to make out the difference here between girls considered too young to marry and those who are already married. The very young girls aren't wearing much of the red ghee and have two uncoloured hair braids pulled forward to cover their eyes, supposedly to keep the evil eye off them. Married women, on the other hand, wear their hair in several thick braids pulled back and wear a little leather ornament on their heads like a tiny crown.

Two old men are sitting open-mouthed and slack-jawed, just staring at the camels. The pair of them are ancient and obviously know every stone and every animal in the vicinity, but camels are new to them. Amazingly, only the women dare to come up and touch one of the animals. The men keep their distance. It's a scenario I will become familiar with over the coming weeks.

I could have stayed here longer getting to know the local people and their way of life but we must be on our way. Even though the women at least look well fed I have to wonder how these people get enough to eat living in such a desolate area. It's been days since we last saw a shop. Later on I learn that they largely live on milk curds and that, after the rains, the animals produce a lot.

The Himba keep telling us how strange they find it to see

white people walking. Up to now the only tourists they've seen have been in cars or a few on motorbikes. They regularly ask our camel herder, who knows their language, 'Where is the white people's car? Or are they so poor that they have to walk everywhere like we do?' A few of them point to the camels and ask, 'Are those their cars?' We find it rather amusing.

The nearer we get to our destination the more often we come across Himba heading the same way. One family is travelling with a donkey or, to be more accurate, the father is riding on the donkey while one child runs behind, one in front, and the donkey itself is laden down with sacks of corn meal and other foodstuffs. Naturally the woman brings up the rear. On another occasion we overtake a young Himba mother striding along with a heavy load on her head, a baby on her back in a sort of rucksack made from goatskin. As we pass this beautiful young woman I can't help noticing a strong rancid smell, almost cer-tainly coming from the red ghee her body is covered in.

Eventually we near our destination, the Epupa Falls. This means once again tackling an unmade track in stifling heat. It's so hot that most of us spend our time fantasising about a cold beer, a cold Coke or just a shady tree to sleep under. And then, all of a sudden, what should materialise in front of us but a bar?

There isn't another building for miles except for this soli-tary bar offering ice-cold drinks. They get their electricity for the fridge from solar panels. Delighted as we are to sit there and knock back a chilled beer, we're also rather disillusioned to know that it's the beer industry subsidising the solar panels to encourage alcohol consumption among the Himba. And behind the building my illusions are shattered further by the sight of a two-metre-high pile of broken bottles.

On the sixth day we reach Epupa and the waterfalls. There is a proper bed waiting for me in our lodgings, which is just heaven. Thanks to the heavy rains a few days ago the water plummeting over the high falls is extraordinarily impressive. It's so loud it's impossible to hear yourself speak.

Looking down on the falls at sunset is a beautiful experience. There are trees growing from crevasses in the rocks jutting up between the rushing water, struggling to find a patch of soil in which to put down roots. The falls are part of the Kunene River, which flows tranquilly into the distance with palm trees along its banks. In the distance bare mountain peaks glisten gold in the setting sun.

The Kunene is the only river here where water flows all year round. There are crocodiles in it and the other bank is Angolan territory. It is not unknown for brave – or perhaps just drunk – tourists to wander across it and never be seen again.

This is the end of the first part of my adventure and my travelling companions – tourists who set out with me on our first warm-up expedition – are returning by minibus to Windhoek the next day. Lucas and I, on the other hand, have to trek back eighty-six kilometres to Okangwati, where we will rendezvous with the expedition leader for the main event. I'm in charge now, but the return journey is a disaster as we have to take a gravel road and are completely devastated by the heat. Every now and then a car will speed past covering us in dust. It's so unbearably hot that I decide we'll get up at 4 a.m. every morning so Lucas and I can load up the camels and be under way before sunrise. But the best thing about these few days is the sense of isolation, and the knowledge that it's all up to me. I also have a chance for more conversation with young Lucas. He's a pleasant lad and over the coming weeks I find him a real source of comradeship, especially when I fall out with the expedition leader.

At one point I ask him if he has a girlfriend and he nods shyly. Knowing that his family don't come from around here, I tease him by asking if she's a Himba. He looks horrified and says, 'Corinne! No. What are you thinking of? Those women don't ever wash and I can't stand that red colour. My girlfriend is modern.'

'So where is she now?' I ask with a laugh.

'Still in kindergarten,' he says without the slightest compunction.

I laugh out loud at this and eventually he joins in too. Eventually he tells me his parents chose her and when she is old enough and he is earning enough money they will get married. It's the custom among his people.

By the time we reach Okangwati, we're exhausted and I absolutely need to put my feet up. The trek back has only made the blisters worse, and some of them have filled up with pus. But I have no intention of giving up my adventure just because of a few blisters. And apart from anything else, I can still hear the expedition leader saying, 'This is no trip for softies and we won't stop just because you get a few blisters.'

Once again, the German couple absolutely spoil me and I do a deal with the guide to let me stay here two days longer so I can celebrate my forty-ninth birthday with them, even if it does mean a slight delay in starting our trip. I spend the days in between walking the dried-up riverbed. While I'm there I come across a few Himba children who are digging a hole and using a cup to fill their plastic canisters with brown, brackish water. It's more or less the same way I had to get water when I lived with the Samburu near Barsaloi. Many a time I would go down to the riverbed, dig a hole and wait for it to fill up so I could wash myself and bring water home to drink. In many ways my life back then resembled that of the Himba here.

The children notice me and start giggling. I say, '*Moro, perivi*' and they reply with '*Naua*', which means 'We're fine'. They stare at my blonde hair and whisper to one another. I sit down next to them and start taking photographs, which I then show them. They're a bit shy at first but soon they overcome their timidity and keep on at me to take more photographs. One of the girls starts dancing, another starts digging furiously so she can see herself doing it in my photographs. I get the impression that a lot of Himba may never have seen themselves in a mirror. Back in Barsaloi lots of the local women would come and squat outside my hut just for the chance to use my hand mirror.

Playing with these kids like this, I'm amazed how happy they are despite their hard lot in life. They laugh together and their eyes sparkle with pure joy. The only one who still seems a bit uncertain about me is the littlest, who can hardly walk. After a while his mother arrives, sits down next to me and starts talking to him, fairly obviously about me. I greet this pretty young woman as I did the children and she smiles. Then she grabs one of the girls and readjusts her skirt to cover her private parts better. I notice that, arranged properly, these short skirts hang in a way that is never revealing, even when they are running and jumping around. She takes hold of the little one and starts washing him, which she does by taking a cup full of water, putting it in her mouth and then spraying it at him. I will never forget the wonderful few hours I spend with these carefree kids in that dried-up riverbed.

To celebrate my birthday I buy a live goat from the Himba for it to be slaughtered and served up as a treat. The children who help out around the place are delighted to be getting some meat. We celebrate my birthday in a small group and enjoy a cold beer afterwards. Tomorrow it's time to be off.

ON MY OWN WITH TWO MEN AND TWO CAMELS

The plan is to set off from Okangwati over Van Zyl's Pass and travel from there along the valley of the Marienfluss River to Red Drum. From there we will go via Orupembe towards Purros to see the desert elephants, then along the Hoarusib River to Opuwo, which is our final destination. That's quite some distance.

We will be walking for six hours every day with just two twenty-minute rest breaks. There is general agreement with my suggestion that we set off around 4 a.m., just as the day dawns, aiming to reach our next campsite between midday and 1 p.m. We set a strenuous pace and I am glad I brought my trekking poles along as they make it much easier. They're particularly useful in the dry riverbeds, where I need all my strength just to keep going. When I ask if we might slow down a bit occasionally, if only to appreciate the landscape more, it only lasts for a brief time. In time I gradually get used to our marching speed but it makes the whole adventure a lot less relaxing. The expedition leader is a big strong type who expects a challenge every day and already knows the whole route. And Lucas is only twenty-two years old and every bit as fit. It's all new to me, though, and I'd prefer not just to be either charging along or falling behind.

Along the route we often come across men with donkeys, which serve as the local equivalent of cars. Occasionally we even see a group of young men dashing along as fast as their beasts can carry them, as if they were showing off their sports cars. On another occasion we pass two old men who seem bewildered as to what we're doing walking the route. One of them appears to be a local chief, or at least it seems like that to me from his proud manner and general appearance. His torso is covered with scars and he's wearing a long necklace of animal teeth. Lucas stops to chat with the pair of them. Despite their age they both have a certain fierce look about them, and they're clearly not happy with something or other. Later Lucas says to me, 'You know what it was? They wanted to know what the camels lived on. They were afraid they would eat all the grass and there'd be none left for their cattle.'

On the third day, just before we reach Van Zyl's Pass, I decide I'm going to study the following day's route and have a talk with the expedition leader as I've decided I want to set off half an hour early each morning, using a head torch if necessary, so I can find my own rhythm, take everything in and get the most out of the journey. Because the one thing that's not in doubt is that the route is absolutely amazing.

So from now on I get up at 3 a.m. and get dressed in my warm tent, which also lets me take the time to deal with my blisters. I put on new plasters every morning. I have two silicon pads, which I strap to my heels to protect them. Then I creep out of the tent, eat the obligatory bowl of muesli made up with powdered milk and dried fruits, and drink a cup of hot tea. I pack up the tent and stow it with the luggage, all still before dawn. As long as the day's route permits, I set out using the head torch until eventually the sun slowly creeps above the horizon and the day proper begins. The extra time I gain by getting up early is the best part of the day. Now and then I disturb a small herd of oryx or other small wildlife. From time to time one thing or another nearly gives me a heart attack, but that just makes the whole experience all the more intense. If it weren't for my experiences in Kenya and the number of times I've gone mountain walking on my own in Switzerland,

I doubt I'd have summoned up the courage to set out alone in the wilderness.

Van Zyl's Pass is an adventure in its own right. It's a hard climb up and takes its toll on the two heavily laden camels. The luggage on their backs keeps slipping and has to be readjusted, which takes up a lot of time. In places the gradient through the pass rises or drops by up to 40 per cent – guidebooks advise only the bravest motorists to attempt it, and in fact vehicles are only permitted to travel from east to west. We come across only two vehicles, both 4x4s, whose drivers look scared out of their wits. The entire pass is thirteen kilometres long.

Climbing our way up the stony streambed is hard enough for us. The camels aren't enjoying it at all, and there are times when I worry about them, particularly going downhill. If one of them were to slip and fall it would almost definitely break a leg. I can only hope and pray it doesn't happen.

At one point a man suddenly appears out of nowhere right in front of me. He's wearing a woolly cap and a headband. His shirt is open, revealing his naked chest adorned with an amulet as well as the usual broad silver neckwear, and he has a stick in one hand and a machete in the other. There's a scar across his face and part of his nose is missing. Obviously he's been attacked and mugged at some point in the past. He just stands and stares as I say hello to him and walk right past.

The vegetation is incredible. Here and there I come across a baobab tree, or something that looks like thick roots with red flowers blooming on them. As we get higher the stone is as dark as granite, but the few leafless trees are almost white. They look like the skeletons of trees.

Just before reaching the top of the pass we pitch camp for the night in a dry riverbed. The camels are pleased and as soon as they are relieved of their burdens start rolling around in the dry sand. It's funny to watch, not least because the frames still fixed to them mean they can't roll over completely, but have to take turns in cleaning first one side and then the other. I go to gather wood for the fire while the two men go off to reconnoitre tomorrow's route so we can work out how to load the camels.

Wherever we pitch our camp it's not long before we get visitors, usually children, but up here on the pass there are also shepherds with their herds of goats or cows. This time it's two curious girls, who just stand there staring at me and, in particular, the camels. I'd like to talk to them but I can't speak Himba and they don't speak English. Instead I hand them some sweets, which brings a big smile to their faces. They take a cautious lick each before popping them into their mouths. Before long their father turns up to join them. He sits himself down on a stone and just watches me. After a while he shoos the girls away and moves closer, which makes me rather uneasy, and I can't help hoping the two men will be back soon. There's something about him that makes me nervous.

I start wondering anxiously if there is something I can do or say to change the atmosphere. He keeps asking me something, but of course I don't understand what he's saying. He seems to be surprised to find me here alone. I'm getting really worried and start fussing about, fetching firewood and making a fire. I go to my tent as if to get the matches and for the first time reach for the pepper spray I brought along to make me feel safer. I slip it into my trouser pocket and come out of the tent holding the matches. This makes me feel a little bit more secure, although I know there's not really anything I could do against a big strong man with a machete. I keep looking up the path towards the pass, praying that the other two will turn up. At last I hear the sound of voices and there they are.

The Himba man who's just been crouching there all this time jumps up. Lucas says something to him, they exchange a few sentences and he heads off in the same direction his children went earlier. I have no idea whether I was misreading the situation or not, but it's the only time I ever felt unsafe in the presence of a Himba man.

Next morning we all set off together and before long we're at the top of the pass. It's very bleak and windy, with only a few tiny trees managing to hold their own against the gale, but the view of the Marienfluss Valley is magnificent: a wide, yellow plain glowing like gold in the sunlight, with the dark silhouettes of the Hartmann Mountains in the distance. We're proud of our camels, even though the hard part, the steep descent, still lies ahead.

I can hardly turn my gaze away from the valley below. The vegetation on either bank of the river cuts like a green band through the yellow grass. Down there is where we'll take our next rest. As we're nearly down to the grasslands we come across a herd of cattle with huge horns who seem as bemused as the locals at the sight of our camels, not sure if they should be afraid or just amazed. Thankfully, the two sets of animals pass one another by without incident. I'm relieved that our two good-natured camels have made it down the steep slope safely.

At the foot of the pass we come across a cluster of stone slabs. At first I think it might be a graveyard but as we get closer and I can read all the inscriptions, I realise they've all been carved by people who've come through the pass by car. The camels need a rest and in any case we need to readjust their loads. As the belt of greenery is our goal, I head down to the riverbed. It's very hot and I can make out a group of ostriches in the tall grass. As I wander along it strikes me that there may be no more Himba this side of the pass, but then all of a sudden I come across two girls on donkeys carrying empty water canisters. It would seem they have to spend a day crossing the pass just to fetch water. Later, Lucas tells me that we'll be lucky to find any water in the coming days, which is why we'll need to ration our 150 litres. Thank God the camels can go for days without water.

The tall thorny grass is so high that when the camels kneel down for us to load them up only their heads and the luggage frames are visible. But every so often we come across circular areas of five to six metres in diameter where there is no grass at all, as if they were UFO landing sites. We plod on and on, but the belt of greenery seems no closer. It is, however, becoming easier to pick out individual peaks in the Hartmann Mountains: flat table tops, soft round hills, and steep peaks.

We spend the next three days walking in parallel with the mountain range without meeting a single human being. I fix upon a point in the distance and simply head for it, for hours on end. For the first time it feels as if I'm walking in a trance. As I plod along the simple sandy path with an unchanging vista of the mountains to one side and an endless emptiness in front of me it suddenly feels as if my body has split into its component parts. My feet move of their own accord and I no longer feel the pain of my blisters. My body sways in rhythm while my arms go up and down with my trekking poles. Bizarrely I feel remarkably happy and eager to go even faster. I'm not even noticing the passage of time. It's only when I get to a place where the path splits and I don't know which way to go that I realise I ought to stop and wait for the others. Even the expedition leader is astonished at the change come over me, and says so. Even when my heel is no more than one huge water-filled blister, once I start going I no longer notice the pain.

Once again the vegetation around us is changing as the land becomes more barren and the ground beneath our feet sandier. The rocky hills are turning red, with great multi-armed cacti jutting out from between the rocks, making for wonderful photo opportunities.

After several days of absolute empty wilderness we begin to come across the occasional settlement. Next to nothing grows here so it's only when I spot some white goats that I realise what they must live on. As we have a planned two-day stop here, the word has already got about that white people are coming and want to 'park' some funny animals here. We're something out of the ordinary for them and lots of the more curious ones just come and watch us for hours on end, which amuses me.

By now we've done a lot of the total trek and I feel quite at one with nature. I could put my tent up and take it down again in my sleep. I only rarely imagine myself back home opening the fridge to take out a slice of ham or a piece of cheese or even a nice big glass of wine. I've lost five kilos, which won't do me any harm.

When we set off again it's only 4.5 kilometres to the Red Drum, the most well-known landmark in the Kaoko Veldt. And in reality it's just what it says it is: a red oil drum sitting out there in the wilderness that is the next best thing to a signpost. Anyone coming by car through here passes this way because it is the point where several of the dirt tracks all meet. Alongside the red drum there is a real signpost that says, 'Marble Campsite: shower and toilet, warm water, 23.5km'. Despite the distance I'm in no doubt that's it's worth the walk just to get a shower. The idea of feeling running water on my body is enough to double my speed. Every now and then along the way a car passes us. Most of them stop briefly to gape at us. The people inside are mostly South Africans but there are a few Germans too. Several of them ask if they can take photographs of us; it would seem we're a tourist attraction in our own right. They can hardly believe how far we've come on foot. For our part, we just plod on through the magnificent landscape, though the one thing in my mind's eye is the shower at the end.

Finally we get there. It's my first shower in ten days. The campsite is in a wonderful location in another dry riverbed. We get to put our tents up in the shade of huge, broad-leafed trees. Even the camels seem to be in a good mood. Each pitch has a fireplace, running water and kitchen equipment. The toilets and washrooms are well kept and built out of local materials so they don't look out of place. The only disappointment is that the cold drinks, much advertised at the reception, are already sold out for today. Still, I suppose you can't have everything. Lucas is happy too because he gets on well with the camp staff and ends up playing football with them.

He's a fan of games of any sort. One evening, as we're sitting round the campfire wondering what to do to pass the time, I suggest a guessing game: each of us will think of an animal we saw on today's trek and the others have to guess what it is. Whoever guesses right goes next. Lucas enjoys the guessing. When it comes to my turn, I think of a chicken we saw in one of the villages we passed through. Lucas makes one guess after another but simply can't get it. Eventually he reckons he's named every single animal we've seen. When I reveal it is a chicken, he gets quite angry and says, 'That's not an animal. A chicken doesn't count. An animal has to have four feet, or else it's not an animal.'

We start laughing and I ask him, 'What is it then?'

'It's a bird, not an animal,' he replies.

We fall about laughing.

'What about snakes?' I ask.

'They're not animals, they're reptiles,' he says. 'Crocodiles have four legs but they're fish because they live in water. And fish aren't animals either.'

For him, that's the end of the discussion. I try to make him see that the word 'animal' includes all of them, but he's not having it. We've spoilt today's game as far as he's concerned.

On another evening we play Boccia together, a simple form of bowls. Lucas and I both select three stones: he has dark ones, I have white ones. We throw a little stone and whoever can land their big stone closest to it wins. He enjoys it at first but soon goes off it when I win, even though all the local Himba children come and watch.

After our R&R at the camp, it's time to set off again, this time for Purros via Orupembe. For much of the way we are walking in the dry bed of the River Khumib. There are lots of tyre tracks, which is good because it's easier to walk in them as the sand has been compressed. I've gone back to getting up before dawn and starting out on my own. My senses are much more aware than normal. Here I hear the slightest noise, and my nose is much more acute. Most mornings there's a trace of wild animal scent along the riverbed. I notice more and more tracks left by animals, giraffes in particular, and the expedition leader warns me that the camels might be frightened by them. He's seen camels run off at the sight of them, taking the loads on their backs with them, and tells me it's no easy matter to get them back again.

I spend part of the morning taking photographs of the riverbed itself, the way it has cracked and split so that in place it looks like neatly arranged shards of pottery. Incredibly there is even the occasional flower glowing bright yellow or pink despite the barren landscape. On one bank I come across an abandoned manyatta, just like the one my African mother-in-law lives in: small and round with walls of cow dung. But apart from two wild donkeys, which have obviously escaped their owners, there's no sign of life.

We weren't wrong about the giraffe tracks though. Shortly after we leave the riverbed to trek along a less strenuous sandy track we find ourselves only a few hundred metres from a family group of four giraffes. We immediately turn the camels' heads away so that they don't see them, and hurry by as fast as we can. But we find ourselves regularly coming across herds of zebra, gazelles and oryx.

The very next evening, however, something weird happens. We're sitting out in the evening sun waiting for the sun to set. The noise of the crickets is deafening and the birds are performing their regular evening concert. Then all of a sudden it is deathly still. Both birds and crickets have gone quiet. All of a sudden everything feels different. I sense this weird feeling inside me and start looking all around. The expedition leader just laughs. Then suddenly the air comes alive and for a few seconds the earth beneath my feet literally moves. It's an earthquake, a small one, but out in the desert it's quite surreal. It takes the animals a long time to get over it. Me too. I spend half the night lying in my tent hoping there isn't an aftershock.

By now we're not too far from Purros. The Atlantic Ocean

is no longer far away. All that lies between us and the coast is fifty kilometres of desert and a small mountain range. Already it's much cooler; the evenings are cold and there's a dampness in the air. One morning we wake up to find ourselves in a mist. Under these circumstances I decide I'd rather not start out on my own, but the expedition leader tells me not to worry: all I have to do is follow the tyre tracks and when they leave the riverbed I should do so too and take the road that runs along the bank. That doesn't sound too difficult so I set off as normal, not least because we have fifteen kilometres to cover on the sand, which I find really difficult, and in any case I'd freeze if I stood around waiting for the men to load up the camels.

Walking in a fog is spooky. Sometimes it lifts a bit and gives me a clearer view, but at other times I can barely make out the track to follow. I start out slowly, still a bit spooked by the fog. There has to be a village of some sort around here, even though I can hardly imagine how the half-naked Himba get by in such cold and damp conditions. After a few kilometres the track diverges from the riverbed and before long I come across a village. It's still very early and I have no idea whether or not the settlement is actually inhabited, so I call out 'Moro' to announce my presence.

There's no response. I can just about see the corral around the village, and the houses, which are square instead of round and almost big enough to stand up in. They don't have any doors so I glance into one, but all there is to see are a few rusty tin cans and a few pots around an extinguished fire. It all looks rather uninhabited, even deserted. The corral is made of thick thorn bushes, not thin twigs as elsewhere, and there's a secondary barrier in the middle, which is obviously a pen for the animals. I'm particularly surprised to see just how many campfires have been lit at some time, an entire circle of them each a few metres from the next. It looks as if they've been lit to fend off wild animals. I can't help wondering if elephants have tried to come through, or if there are lions in the area.

The cold's beginning to seep into my bones so I march on.

It can't be long now before the men catch up with me. The
track begins to lead uphill, which is rather disconcerting, as
I thought it ran alongside the river. There's a fierce wind and
I'm starting to freeze. I stop and wait for twenty minutes but
nobody shows up. I call out, but there's no answer. Then suddenly the fog lifts and I can see the greenery nearly a kilometre away and start to panic, realising I must have veered
away from the riverbed too early. I run back as fast as I can
towards the river, using the emergency whistle in my back-
pack, but the wind carries the sound in the opposite direction.
When I get back to the riverbed, I find my own tracks but
also those of the camels, indicating that my companions have
already passed by. I've got no idea how far they've gone by now
and I find myself weeping tears of anger, disappointment and
pure terror. I've almost never felt quite so alone. Then all of a
sudden the pair of them appear out of the fog. They'd turned
back to look for me.

As the day goes on, the fog begins to lift and before long
everything is back to normal: blue sky, hot sun and dry earth.
Everywhere around us there are abundant signs of life, from
funny little round bushes growing out of the sand to little
white flowers with overlarge leaves growing amid the stones.
At one point a chameleon jumps out in front of me, and stops
dead, his eyes alone moving, swivelling in his head.

But gradually the golden grass and the beautiful flowers
make way to stone wilderness, flanked by bare, sandstone-
coloured mountain ranges. The stony ground beneath our feet
is hard, and there's been no fresh grass for the camels for a
while now, so they have to eat the food we brought with us. The
route on to Purros is among the hardest we have encountered:
just stony desert with tracks that undulate like a washboard
straight ahead as far as the eye can see. There's no way we can
find a place to stop here: there's no shade and the stones are
too heavy to move to find somewhere to sit. I'm beginning to
find the trek too much for me.

Then all of a sudden a car comes up and the expedition

leader stops it to ask if they'll give me a lift as far as Purros. He and Lucas will catch up with me twenty-four kilometres further on. Considering we've already been walking for six hours, I accept the offer without the slightest hesitation. I doubt I'm going to be missing much, and I don't envy my male companions – or the camels – for a second.

The people in the car are an elderly English couple who are good company and very kind hosts. Given that all my luggage is packed on one of the camels, they take me to the campsite and lend me a towel, shower gel and something to eat. We have a good old chat and they're amazed what I've done, especially when they see the state of my feet. The woman in particular is horrified and gives me some medicinal cream and some normal plasters which stay on better.

Once again the campsite is simple but nice. Each pitch has a place to make a fire, running water, a shower and basic toilet. The English couple offer me a cup of tea but just as we're about to drink it, my male companions arrive with the camels after what must have been a real forced march. We're delighted to accept the English couple's invitation to join them for dinner.

We stay in the camp for three days. There are signs that point out we are in the middle of a wilderness and that elephants and other wild animals might wander into the campsite. We're ordered not to leave any fruit or other foodstuffs lying around in our tents, even though the guards tell us they don't think there are any elephants around. They haven't been here for several weeks and are almost certainly up near the Hoarusib River, which might have water flowing now. That's where we're headed for next.

The village of Purros sits in the middle of a desert surrounded by mountains that continually change colour. The landscape is beautiful and, as we're here for a few days, I ask to go and see the village, which is four kilometres away. Lucas and the expedition leader are busy talking to a Japanese guy who came here specially to see the desert elephants and has been waiting in vain for five days, so I set out on my own. The track splits in two just before it reaches the riverbed, and I decide to take the shady path and cross over a bit further on. The trees here are enormous and there are lots of strange root formations, which make great photographic subjects.

I'm busy taking a photograph of one of them when I look up and find myself face to face with a huge tusked elephant quietly munching on a tree. My heart leaps. I take a quick bit of video and three photographs before running back to the campsite. I can't wait to share my experience. There's a big grin all over my face: for the first time I've come face to face with a desert elephant without a fence between me and him or a car to escape in.

But the campsite is empty. They've all gone off to Purros and from the tracks in the sand I can tell they've already crossed the riverbed. I'm not brave enough to go back to take another look at the behemoth I came across so instead I set off to Purros myself. The village is run down and not exactly charming. The only reason people come here is to see the elephants. There's a little runway outside town for tourists who choose to fly in rather than make the strenuous journey in a 4x4.

There's no sign of the others so I make short work of my visit and head back. I'm not far from where I was when I came across the elephant when I spot a couple of giraffes peering out from a bush on the other side of the river. It's simply amazing to be able to see so many animals living in the wild just while wandering along on foot.

Later that evening I show the others the photographs and the video that I took that day and the Japanese man can't believe his bad luck. That same evening he books himself on to a guided jeep tour and finally manages to see some elephants down on the riverbed.

The camels are rested, have at last had some water and God knows how many kilos of some sort of bean-like fodder. It's time for us to be off again. We need to stick together as we walk along the Hoarusib as there might be lions here and I'd rather not be their breakfast. It would appear that the scent of the camels puts them off.

The riverbed is incredibly wide and it's not hard to imagine floods of water rushing by in the rainy season. There are bushes several metres high along the banks. A few trees grow out of the river and we come across roots protruding from the bed. The sun takes its time rising and gives a soft red and gold glow to everything. We stop on some high ground to look back at Purros and at the tall hedge of palm trees ahead of us. That's where the first water is to be found in the riverbed at present, even if initially it's just a trickle. But gradually it gets wider and we leave the track and walk alongside this famous river. There are tyre tracks to follow which makes the route easier as otherwise the sand is too fine and deep and would pour into our walking shoes, turning the insoles into sandpaper.

We keep coming across evidence of elephants using the same route: either huge oval footprints or giant heaps of dung. They look dry, suggesting that the animal passed by several days ago. Now there is an increasing flow of water reflecting the palms along the banks. There are more plants growing around and in the water, which makes it harder to know just how far away the elephants are. But before long we come across some fresh dung and more footprints. It feels weird to know there are elephants somewhere nearby but not to be able to see them. Lucas says he's not too comfortable with it either, and that only makes me more nervous. Our expedition leader is driving the camels on while checking his GPS to make sure we don't go the wrong way in this wide and wandering waterway.

All of a sudden I can smell the elephants, and my heart is pounding. The two men seem on edge too. Only the camels keep on plodding along calmly. Now and then we spot a grey elephant's head either on the right behind the bushes or on the left behind us. It's really exciting to see them, but it would be nice if they weren't quite so close.

I have to work hard to keep up with the men. Lucas keeps turning round to wave to me to come closer. But no matter how much I try, I just can't walk any faster on this sand. If I tried any harder, I'd be exhausted in no time. We're just coming round a huge patch of bushes when all of a sudden we hear a loud snort, and immediately change direction. Then, just a couple of hundred metres away, I spot a mother elephant with two little ones. It's a charming sight but we can't linger because we have to put some distance between her and us. It's a bit of an adrenalin buzz, but at the same time I can't help thinking we must be mad to do this with no more protection than a couple of camels.

Then I spot another elephant standing on a little hillock under a palm tree. It occurs to me, as we hurry on away from him, that he might be the alpha male. We turn the next corner and quite unexpectedly come across a group of people fetching water from the river. Almost immediately they all climb up on to the riverbank and begin banging their metal cups together in warning. I'm wondering if all this fuss is just because of our camels, when all of a sudden the expedition guide calls out to me, 'Corinne, watch out, there's a bull elephant making straight towards us. We need to get out of the riverbed and get the camels to safety. Run for it.'

I look up and immediately see a huge elephant coming towards me, picking up speed. He may be some two hundred metres away still, but he looks like he can cross that distance in no time. I need to get out of the car tracks to change direction, but as soon as I do, I find I can hardly move. I lean as hard as I can on my trekking sticks and manage to drag myself metre by metre towards the riverbank and the safety of the trees. Behind me I can hear people hurling stones at the elephant, who has already spread his ears wide in an attacking posture. I'm spluttering and can hardly move. The camels are already out of sight behind the trees by the time I finally get myself out of the sand and can move at any speed. I glance back and see that the elephant has changed direction and is heading straight for the little hill. The people standing there are banging stones against their metal cups, making a huge din. Just as I reach the relative safety of the trees, I notice a Herero woman standing on another little hill waving at me, presumably urging me on. But to me it seems eerily spooky, as if she were a scarecrow.

At last I'm back with my companions, who are every bit as worked up as I am, particularly Lucas. Sitting round the campfire later he tells me that was the first time he'd seen an elephant close up. He'd never particularly wanted to, not least because he'd lost his father to an elephant attack.

For the next stage of the trek we keep to the riverbank in the hope that we see any wild animals sooner from there. But even here we keep coming across elephant footprints and dung piles. Now and again I spot ape tracks that look just like the marks from human hands and feet. We continue for a few hours and then decide to pitch camp. It's the most nerve-racking night of the whole trip for me. The next day Lucas tells me he didn't get a wink of sleep either. Our expedition leader was the only one to snore all through the night.

In the morning I notice that once again the landscape has changed completely. It's much hillier now and there is yellow grass everywhere. We regularly come across springboks leaping across the trail. It's great fun watching them, especially when they take enormous leaps into the air. And yet again the trail leads us along a riverbed, although this one is much narrower which means the water is deeper. Eventually we find ourselves in what is almost a canyon with red stone walls rising on either side, sometimes in extraordinary shapes. Every now and then a white tree clings to the rocks, and from time to time we come across tall palm trees that look as if they've been deliberately planted there. It's much cooler here, but the camels don't particularly like it because the water is flowing faster and the sand is wet and damp. We keep having to push and pull them to keep them on the move. The expedition leader decides we're going to have to change our route because the water is too fast-flowing here for us to continue. That means a detour of another eighty kilometres and going back along part of the route we've already covered. But you can't fight nature.

The new route means we have to cross hilly country on the edges of the Etendeka mountain range, but as an experienced hill walker I'm more than happy with that. It also means we come across mountain zebras, just a small family group, but the male is a particularly impressive specimen. I've never seen a zebra with such a thick, flowing mane. They're in general much darker in colour than the zebras you find on the steppe lands. They're also a lot more wary. One glance at us and they're off, at a gallop.

The land here is stony and barren. It's been days since we've come across any people. Every now and then we come across abandoned huts or a tree with obvious human markings on it. I would like to come across a few more of the jolly Himba women. We pitch camp under one of the huge trees that seem to be common around here. I climb up a nearby hill to appreciate what a pretty picture our little campsite makes, with its green canopy standing out in this sparse landscape, the white Iglu tents underneath and a smoking fire with a black cooking pot hanging over it.

We have to retrace our steps through the foggy stretch and go right past the place where I got lost. It all looks a lot less scary now as the fog has mostly gone, as has the biting wind. We spend two days walking along the Khumib riverbed and then take the track that leads to Opuwo. Once again I start out early on my own to enjoy the dawn and the silence, broken only by the birdsong that greets the morning. We've still got one hundred and fifty kilometres to go by the time we come across a Himba village again. I realise we're near because I spot a lad with a large herd of brown and white goats. Shortly afterwards I come across three huts that look just like manyattas, but in fact are built mostly out of leather. Given that the Himba are mostly nomadic shepherds, I reckon these are only temporary structures. There's smoke coming from one of the huts and a few goat kids running around.

A little further on I spot a bigger, proper village and hang on for my companions to catch up with the camels, because I love seeing the way the Himba react to these unfamiliar animals. I'm not disappointed: six Himba women come running up to us, their naked breasts bouncing up and down. When they see the camels they stop and stare while Lucas chats to them. We don't see any men, though, and when I think about it I'm amazed at how few men we come across at all.

The closer we get to our destination the more individual huts or little settlements we find along the way. In one of them we even come across a little shop and indulge in our first soft drink in weeks. Everywhere we go the people stare at us and a few call out to me, though I can't understand what they are saying. I ask Lucas to translate for me and he says, 'They're telling you to watch out for the leopards living in the hills around here.' I thank my lucky stars I haven't come across one.

We don't come across many cars but I still have the impression that they get more tourists here, if only because the Himba are more reticent about talking to us. Out in the savannah I spot two little coloured roofs and a metal fence next to a tree. These turn out to be the first graves we have seen. It would appear that these are the graves of Himba converted by missionaries because each has an inscription and a cross on it. People have left cow horns next to them. After the empty wasteland we've spent weeks trekking through this all seems out of place to me.

We're about to set up camp one evening after yet another long trek along a dried-up riverbed when all of a sudden a host of baboons leaps, screeching and howling, out of the water and up on to some nearby rocks. It's incredibly impressive to see so many of them all at once, but it can be dangerous too. But luckily for us they throw the little ones on to their backs or under their bellies and run off, leaving behind them however a huge mess of dung.

The area is particularly picturesque and there is cool shade beneath the high rocks. I lie down outside my tent, as I often do when we've pitched camp for the night, and my thoughts drift back to my home in Switzerland. Not having mobile phones, music or seeing the news allows me to enjoy being where I am. Once a week I make a satellite call to my daughter, just to let her know I'm still alive. She worries so much about me.

She will be twenty in five days' time and I rather regret that I can't be with her to drink a toast on such an important occasion. But at least I can speak to her on the sat phone. I'm still trying to work out what I'm going to do with myself once this great adventure is over. The one thing clear to me is that I'm not going to get over my obsession with Africa, no matter whereabouts in the world I find myself. Africa is in my heart and I feel totally at home among the people here, especially the herders and other nomads. The fascination they exert over me shows yet again just how important my time living with the Samburu was to me, and how lucky I was to have been able to share their primitive lifestyle for four long years alongside my husband, the Samburu warrior Lketinga.

Next morning, however, my mind is back on the day's long march. We set off very early and pass a little village where everything is silent and there's nobody to be seen. Even the goats and cattle are just lying there dozing. Only the dogs wake up and bark at us. But by midday we're surrounded by curious onlookers, including lots of children who wear nothing but a chain slung around their waists and below their plump little tummies, and an amulet around their necks. Usually the children hide behind the women and peek out at us. One of the women reaches out her arm and walks cautiously towards the camels. A man tells her off, but she pays no heed to him and starts gently stroking the underside of the camel's neck. Another Himba woman, with huge breasts the size of watermelons hanging down over her belly, copies her. Once again I'm impressed by the older women who still paint themselves from top to tail with the ochre colouring used by the young women. It gives them a sort of magic aura.

It's time for us to move on, so we say our goodbyes. The road heads gently uphill from here on, into giraffe country. It's a beautiful landscape, remarkably green, with clumps of bushes all over the place. One herder comes towards us with his goats and his daughter, a pretty young girl, riding on a donkey next to him. Her face is almost completely hidden by the thick braided plaits hanging down over her eyes. She's wearing the traditional Himba silver neckband and an ornate white belt around her waist. I've seen such a belt before, on little girls as young as seven years old. It's a sign to indicate she is spoken for. Often, because they are betrothed so young, they end up wearing the belt until they are old enough to be married. But then sometimes they are married as young as ten, although it is not to be consummated until they begin menstruating. At least, thank God, they don't undergo female genital mutilation, which the Samburu and Masai still inflict on their women. And even though they are married off so young, most of them seem happy enough.

The sight of all these goats reminds us that it's been a while since we've eaten any meat. But this herder will not sell any of his animals. The next day, however, we have a bit more luck. We get to a village where all the goats are penned next to the houses. As usual, all the women and children come out to see us and, after we've exchanged greetings and a bit of chat, Lucas asks about buying one of the goats. There's a bit of a discussion and then a man in a T-shirt, long trousers and a hat appears. It would appear the animals belong to him. He points out two that he is willing to sell.

After a bit of haggling we buy one of them and decide to camp for a couple of days by the riverbed not far from the village. Lucas has a hard time trying to get the goat to leave the rest of the herd and come with us, and I'm starting to feel guilty. But the animal's former owner lends him a hand to drag the animal away from the others and slaughter it with a machete. We've promised him he can hold on to the pelt and innards. Lucas makes a good job of butchering the carcass and within an hour there are chunks of meat hanging from higher tree branches where the dogs can't get at them. I start chopping one of the hunks into smaller pieces, which I throw into a big pot on the fire. Fresh goat meat can be tough, something we discover when we try to roast and eat one of its hind legs.

Before long a few women from the village come over and sit slightly away from our tents and watch us. A few of them go down to the riverbed and fill a canister with water before coming over to us. Nearly all of them have a baby in their arms or at their breast. A few boys and girls play around in the bushes, chasing off monkeys looking for nuts. There's a log of giggling and tittering and a lot of very obvious staring at our meat hanging on the branches. They spend a couple of hours with us, chatting away with Lucas. There's laughter and earnest discussion. I ask Lucas what they're talking about and he says, 'I shouldn't really tell you, but they're crazy for meat and would do anything to have some of it.' I'm ready to cut some down and give it to them, but the expedition leader won't have it.

Gradually it gets dark and the men come to fetch their women. To our surprise the women shoo them away. I can't help being impressed by the way the women stand up for one another, laughing together as they do so. Eventually, however, they realise that our expedition leader won't change his mind and slope off with disappointed expressions. I sympathise with them. A few of them go to refill their water canisters before they load the children on to their backs, the canisters on to their heads and set off back to the village.

Next day a few of the girls and women come out again to see us. Once again they sit down and start trying to persuade us to give them some meat. Eventually our expedition leader reluctantly gives them the hind leg that we're not going to eat anyhow. Obviously there isn't enough to go round and in the end he chops up a bit more and shares it out. At last the women are satisfied and do a dance for us that gradually gets more and more frenetic. They form a circle and one by one take it in turns to stand in the middle of it, the woman in the centre spinning round and stomping her feet while the others clap and sing. After a few twirls another one takes her place in the middle, and all the time they're laughing, screaming, chanting and clapping and stamping faster and faster. After a while there's a cloud of dust spinning around them and their red braids are spinning around their heads, and their little skirts flying high, though they manage to take care to cover their private parts, even if their bare bottoms are exposed. I ask the expedition leader if this is a normal part of the dance, or if they're trying to encourage him to hand out a bit more meat.

Lucas is enjoying it all, laughing out loud and describing the flashing parade or rear ends as 'crazy'.

'They're not really human beings at all,' he says.

I ask him what he means by that and he says, 'Just look at them. They don't act like human beings, running around half-naked, covering their bodies with that red fat, never washing their hair. And then you know it's one of their traditions to knock out their front four teeth and then laugh at us and call us dogs, because we have "mouths full of teeth".'

I can't help laughing at the nonsense he comes out with, and yet I have to acknowledge that the local customs vary hugely from tribe to tribe.

By now the women are tired out from the dancing, with beads of sweat rolling down their faces. They sit down and tuck into the chunks of meat, finishing it all off before going home. They obviously fear their menfolk would take it off them. Gradually, they drift off one by one, wrapping the little children in the goatskin backpacks and disappearing towards the village. The expedition leader and Lucas take the camels down to the river so that they can stock up on water before we set out the next morning on the final stage of our trek.

I'm sitting there outside my tent looking at the photos I've taken when all of a sudden three big male apes charge into the campsite. Two of them leap over my head to climb the tree where our meat is hanging, while the other smashes into the tent. I leap up in shock, grab my trekking poles and wave them towards them. They shout and scream but make no move to run off. They snarl at me, showing their teeth and staring at me with their yellowy-brown eyes as if challenging me. I'm not sure if it's the meat they want or something else. I'm standing there wondering what to do when a Himba man comes up from the river, carrying his machete. One look at him and the apes swing up into the trees and flee. They obviously weren't as worried about a female, despite the sticks I was waving at them. It was only the sight of a male human that scared them off. I thank my rescuer and give him a little bag of tobacco, which he accepts with thanks. I look round and can now see the whole troop of apes sitting on the ground or hanging from the palm trees watching us. Yet even though there have been signs of apes or baboons around ever since we got here, within the hour every one of them has vanished.

Our trek is coming to its end. We're only fifty kilometres from Opuwo and, as we plod on, I'm gradually beginning to look forward to getting back to 'civilisation'. Even Lucas is starting to get excited. The end of the tour means it's holiday time for him and he can go back to his family in the Damara region with the money he's earned. But the expedition leader has one more stop planned. Our final campsite is in a savannah landscape not far from a waterhole. I take the opportunity to walk down to it to wash my hair and clothes so that I'm not too grubby by the time we get back to Opuwo.

Today is my daughter's birthday and I've been looking forward to talking to her on the sat phone. But I'm devastated to find that the battery's dead. I have solar cells to recharge it, but it'll take hours. Just sitting there doing nothing waiting for the battery to charge leaves me feeling rather melancholy.

It's also twenty years since I was living out there in northern Kenya far from civilisation, just like right now. Except at that moment I was in a rustic hospital up in Wamba waiting for my child to be born. I knew nothing about childbirth. Before coming to Africa I hadn't even thought about it. My mother-in-law spoke only the local Maa language and my husband wasn't up to telling me anything about the process of giving birth: that was women's stuff. I had no pre-natal course, knew nothing about exercising during pregnancy, never had an ultrasound. I could only wait, hope and pray that, despite the circumstances, my child would be born alive and healthy. Twenty years ago today, despite having three bouts of malaria while I was pregnant, I managed to give birth to a healthy little girl.

All of this is running through my head as I sit waiting and waiting with nothing else to do. Finally there is enough charge in the battery to make a call and I try to ring my little girl and wish her a happy birthday. At last I get through to her in Zurich and I could jump for joy, even if she tells me she can't talk for long as things are hectic back there and she has to be off to work.

I spend the rest of the day coming to terms with the end of my adventure. We only have two more days to go and I'm both happy and sad to be coming to the end. There is still a long hard trek before then, and so I finally apply the last of my sticking plasters to the huge blisters on my feet.

The final part of our journey is on a broad but hard track that's not very pleasant to walk on. I set off alone early, walking as fast as I can. Now there are more and more cars along the way. Some of the drivers are locals who wave at me in astonishment, some tourists who slow down and stop and ask if I'm in difficulty. I just smile and tell them no, and point back at the camels coming along behind me. They're usually astounded and want to know where we've been. Some of them even get out of their vehicles to be photographed alongside me. The one thing I hear more often than most is, 'You have to be Swiss to do something that daft!'

There are more and more signs of civilisation now along the way. For the last couple of weeks we've seen electricity poles indicating that Opuwo, capital of the Kaoko Veldt, is not far away. Funnily enough, in the Himba language Opuwo means 'end', which makes it a fitting place to finish our 720km trek.

I'm exhausted but proud and almost light-headed as people crowd round me and the two men and two camels as we trudge into this tiny town of just five thousand people. We fell like we've finally reached civilisation, even if for those in the national capital, Windhoek, Opuwo really is the end of the world!

A NEW CHALLENGE BACK IN KENYA

Mid-July 2009, much enriched by my experiences, and twelve kilograms lighter, I arrive back in Ticino Canton, Switzerland. After eight weeks in a landscape that's been either wild or barren, the sight of the lush green meadows adorning the mountains as I take the train from Zurich back to my home in Lugano is one for sore eyes. The next day, without even unpacking my suitcase, I pack up a little rucksack and head up into the mountains, reaching 2,200 metres, where I find myself among the last remnants of the winter snows. The contrast with the trek I've just completed is almost unbelievable: all around me are meadows full of wild flowers, the alpenroses red against the grey rocks and the blue sky. My recent experience makes me appreciate all this more than ever. The perfume of the flowers is so sweet, it almost makes me light-headed. Yesterday I was in Namibia; today I'm back home in the Alps. Our world has so much to offer.

Over the next few months I do a lot of mountain walking, just letting my thoughts run wild. At one moment I'm back in the Namibian desert with the unique Himba, the next I'm back in Kenya with my family there. Napirai has finally said she would like to meet them, although I'm not sure she is really ready. It's six years since I was last there and I'd love to go again, but I can't go back without taking my daughter with me. There would be no way I could explain her absence to her father or grandmother who long to see her again.

At the same time I've been knocked out of my old routine by my trip to Namibia and my curiosity about Kenya has been reawakened. I would really love to find out just what it is about Africa that sparks this sense of energy in me every time I set foot on the continent. It is a sensation that goes against virtually everything we are told about Africa here in Europe. Most of the people I know who have been to Kenya or any other African country just want to understand how the people there manage to survive.

There is also the fact that if I were to get the chance to meet as many people as possible and hear their life stories then I might have something of interest to share with my readers. I've had so many letters and emails telling me how much their lives have been influenced by reading my story. Surely hearing more about people who have to struggle against the worst conditions and still not lose their love of life would give them even more strength and confidence?

The only question is, how am I going to find such stories? By happy coincidence Klaus, the cameraman who went with me when I returned to Barsaloi six years ago, is planning to fly out to Nairobi for several weeks with his Kenyan wife and their daughter. When I tell him what I'm thinking about, he suggests I join them, and tells me he can introduce me to all the people he's got to know in Nairobi over the intervening years. He can put me in touch with people who have struggled to get by against incredible odds. Immediately I'm fired up with enthusiasm and accept the offer gratefully.

By the end of February I'm off to Africa again, this time to Nairobi, capital of Kenya. It's not exactly my favourite city in the world, but I have the feeling it's the right place to go to. I have no idea as yet that the fascinating tales I am going to bring back will finally overcome Napirai's uncertainty and give her the courage and inspiration she needs to go back to Barsaloi with me just a few months later.

The centre of Nairobi is very modern and smart, with luxury apartment buildings everywhere and rents that are almost as high as they are in Germany. There are new supermarkets on every corner, and even the modern automotive industry has finally made its presence felt. I'm amazed to see how many expensive top-end, brand-new cars there are on the busy streets of Nairobi. Only a few years ago there was a beggar in rags on every corner cadging money off tourists. Not any more. I can't help wondering what they've done with them all. There's no rubbish on the streets and it looks as if everybody has stopped smoking. It's hard to believe how much the city centre has changed.

I've rented a flat in the centre of town for four weeks. By Kenyan standards it's more than adequate, even if it's not quite what we might expect in Europe. I have to climb six flights of stairs every day to get to my apartment as there's no lift. I also have to bring in my own drinking water as Nairobi tap water isn't recommended for delicate European stomachs. The furniture is a bit rundown and the plaster is peeling from the walls in places. The shower isn't reliable all through the day as the water struggles to make its way up to the higher floors. I fill up a bucket before I shower so that I can at least be sure of rinsing the shampoo out of my hair when I wash it. I can't rely on the toilet either and find myself calling in a plumber every three to four days. In the little kitchen I have a fridge and an old gas cooker with a rather dodgy burner. But in the living room there's a television and a powerful music system. There's a cleaner who comes in daily and when things go wrong the concierge tries to sort them out.

There's even an outdoor swimming pool, which given the general shortage of water in Nairobi is a real luxury. But most important of all is the fact that we have a twenty-four-hour porter on the door, which means that no uninvited guests can get into the gated area. But then that's almost always the case in the better-off parts of Nairobi. Depending on which company he works for a porter-cum-guard can earn between €80 and €120 a month. When you take into account that I'm paying

€740 a month rent for a one-bedroom apartment, it makes you wonder what the conditions must be like where the porter lives. But by and large I'm comfortable here. Later on, when I've spent days on end in the slums, climbing up six floors to my simple little room feels like living in the lap of luxury.

The day after we arrive Klaus and I head out to find a market so I can get that typically African hectic buzz I love so much. We find one on a large area of land not too far out of the city centre. I wander among the stalls where the locals sell fruit and vegetables laid out attractively on simple trestle tables. Some of the sellers have simply laid out tomatoes on the ground, selling them for a few cents. Then we come to a fish stall with big deep-fried fish laid out next to one another neatly on brown paper. The stallholder has lit a fire on the ground and is using a wok to fry the fish in oil until they go crispy. She's doing great business with people queuing up to carry away their purchases wrapped up in newspaper. It smells great and makes me salivate just to look at it.

For the moment I wander on, taking in the colourful scene. We come across the second-hand section of the market where there are huge piles of shoes, clothes and handbags – in fact, almost anything you can imagine is on sale. All the clothes are clean and each item has been ironed. Obviously I get pestered to buy something as they all reckon they can do a good deal with a white person. I reply with a smile and say I'll take a look later. It's amazing just how much there is on offer, but for today I'm happy enough to soak up the atmosphere. One or two of the sellers have sprawled out on top of their pile of wares to take a midday siesta. We leave the 'clothing department' behind us and come across the vegetable wholesale department. The ground here is a real quagmire and we're thankful we put on wellington boots. One of the stalls is already sold out and the plump woman in charge is lying on the ground taking the money from her employees. It's a great sight: I can't imagine how anyone back in Europe would react to see a shop owner lying down among their cabbages and tomatoes.

Behind her I notice there are a couple of cows chomping away on bits of discarded greenery. There's music coming from behind what purports to be a little teahouse, but looks like a rather dilapidated shack. I tiptoe up to it and suddenly find myself looking at an open-air church service. It's amazing: everybody up and dancing around a little square in front of a pastor and a musician playing on a keyboard. The speakers have been cobbled together and the sound is more than a little tinny, but the dancers are all swaying together devoutly, clapping their hands and singing along to the melody.

A little further I come across a ditch full of dirty water and just beyond it what appears to be an ironing shop. I can't get over the sight of a forty-something man standing there with a makeshift ironing board and an antediluvian iron filled with hot charcoal, ironing a white shirt so carefully that not one speck of charcoal falls out to dirty it. I ask him if he minds me sitting watching him for a while. He's more than happy and points to a bench clearly intended for customers to sit while they wait. He tells me proudly, still ironing away, that this is his own business and he has two employees, indicating the two younger men behind him, also busy ironing. He's been doing this for five years, having built up the business on his own. He uses one hand to show off the premises: walls made from a few empty maize sacks hanging from hails, a sheet of plastic as a roof to keep off the sun. He admits that he can't iron when it's raining because it won't quite keep out the rain. The ironing boards are broad planks of wood set up on plastic stands. The little makeshift shop which accommodates all three of them is barely three metres by five – or, ten foot by sixteen.

It might seem random to my Swiss way of looking at the world, but it works well. More and more customers keep coming in while I sit there. Somebody brings in a dress to be ironed, another woman hands over five skirts she wants to sell in the second-hand market. I ask him how business is and he says, 'Not bad. I get a lot of custom from the second-hand clothes market and some days I end up ironing six hundred items. I start at 8 a.m. and work until 6 p.m. After that it's too dark.'

Good grief, I'm thinking to myself: ironing six hundred items with that ancient heavy old iron. Back home people moan if they have to iron one basket of washing with our super-light modern steam irons. But here's this man who's just proud that he's managed to get hold of more than one basic iron and been able to hire two employees. 'I get between three and twenty shillings per item,' he tells me. 'But I have to give ten shillings a day to the Masai for them to look after the place at night. They graze their cattle just over there. They make good nightwatchmen and would defend the shops here with their lives. There are more than a hundred shops here and they all pay them the same. Then it costs another hundred shillings a month to rent the spot. I pay my assistants half what I charge per item.'

When I think that 100 Kenyan shillings is just €1, those seem ludicrously small sums. But things are different here.

I'm amazed to watch him slip several skirts one under the other, lay a damp cloth on top of them and pick up a different, much heavier iron from the ground. He explains to me: 'You need a different type of iron depending on the fabric. I have to use a really heavy, very hot iron for cotton, but I have a lighter one for silk. To get the iron really hot I put a couple of tin cans over it. That acts like a sort of oven that heats up the charcoal even more but makes the iron lighter.'

He beams at me and suggests I might like to have a go. I'm not so sure this is a good idea: you need to hold a wet cloth over the handle even to hold the iron and I'm not certain I could make sure none of the charcoal falls on to the clean washing. I explain why I'm a bit afraid, and he just says, 'Hakuna matata – it's not hard, you'll manage.' Reluctant to disappoint him I get up, go over to the ironing board and pick up the iron. I can hardly believe how heavy it is: it has to weigh at least two kilograms. There's absolutely no way I could make that thing glide smoothly and easily over the clothing laid out. It's hard enough to do just a few centimetres and the three of them burst out laughing when I give up. I laugh along with them but start coughing. All of a sudden the ironing man gets serious and tells me: 'It's not a healthy job. You spend all day breathing in charcoal dust. I'm forty-two years old and I can't keep on doing it for much longer. Some days I can't catch my breath. But I have a wife and two children to feed. We're having a church wedding next week,' he says proudly.

'Why now?' I ask.

'Because a wedding costs a lot of money. All the relatives want to come. I'll have to provide food and drink for over a hundred people and lots of them will need putting up because they have to come a long way to get to Nairobi. But after being married for ten years, I've scraped the money together and want to do this for my wife,' he says with a smile of satisfaction spread across his face.

I wish him all the best and congratulate him. I could see from the moment I laid eyes on him that this was a good and honest man. As far as I can tell from the nearly three hours I've spent sitting here watching him work, the customers seem to like him too. I take my farewell, delighted to have made the acquaintance of such a hard-working, good-natured man who clearly loves his wife and is satisfied with his simple lot in life.

With a spring in our step after such an uplifting experience we make our way back through several muddy ditches to where we parked the car. A few days later I find myself thinking of the ironing man again and tell myself never to grumble when I have to do the ironing: all I need to do is plug it in and the work, by comparison, practically does itself.

GREENERY IN THE MIDST OF THE SLUMS

Klaus has organised a meeting for me with the French charity foundation Solidarité, which provides self-help assistance for Nairobi's slum dwellers. One of their projects is to teach people to grow their own vegetables in big plastic bags filled with soil. In a slum where nobody has a garden because there simply isn't any space, it sounds like a brilliant idea. I'm eager to hear more about it, to go and see the project itself and meet the people enrolled in it.

We turn up at the headquarters of the organisation, introduce ourselves, and a bubbly female agriculture scientist explains the programme to me and then spontaneously volunteers to take us out on a tour of the slums the next day to see it in action.

The next morning we head for Kibera, the biggest slum in all of Kenya. In Nairobi alone there are more than two hundred districts classified as slums, which are home to more than half the city's population. Kibera stretches over three square kilometres, and is home to several hundred thousand people. You can imagine how closely they live to each other. Nobody has any privacy. Only a few shacks have electricity and everybody has to fetch their water in canisters. There's on average just one toilet for several hundred people. If the queues are too long they have to use plastic bags to relieve themselves. Kibera is effectively a city within a city, with its own rules and regulations. Each and every inhabitant is concerned only with day-to-day survival. Today I'm going to meet some of them and hear their life stories.

There are four of us altogether; it's not advisable for 'white people' to visit unaccompanied. Apart from anything else it would be easy to get lost in among so many similar tin shacks and never find a way out again. The first thing we have to do is register our presence with the district officer in order to get official permission to enter Kibera. We have to show our papers and enter our names and addresses in a visitors' book. Before leaving we will have to come by again and register that we have left so the district officer knows nobody has simply disappeared. We then plod on foot through an ankle-deep morass of dirt, mud and excrement. I'm glad I've remembered my wellies. I'm going to need them.

Antony, from criminal to gardener

First of all we go to see a group of young men who make a living from the so-called 'Gardens in a Sack'. They are lucky enough to have a piece of land outside the slum, close to the main road. Even so, it's very noisy and there's a perpetual stink of exhaust fumes. Every few seconds some hulking great lorry rattles past. I can see, even as we come on to their land, that the young men in question are hard at work. Some of them are digging up soil while others are collecting little stones. There are loads of big white sacks with greenery growing from them scattered about. I'm introduced to Antony, who is twenty-eight years old and seems to be the group leader, even though officially there is no such thing. He's of average height with muscular arms and a red cap on his head. He's going to tell me what they do here and why.

'You have to know, Corinne,' he starts by saying, 'before we got the chance to earn a living like this, we were all thieves and layabouts. We stole anything we could and even our neighbours didn't trust us. But what can you do when your stomach is growling with hunger? Most of us were drug users as a way to overcome our misery. A few of us had even been to school up to leaving age, but still couldn't find a job. I wasn't bad in school, even if I was born in a slum, as was my mother before me. I lived in a tiny hut with her and five brothers and sisters. I never knew my father. It's the same for lots of lads around here. You all get together, form a gang. There were about fifty of us altogether, though not all of them are still alive. About twenty were gunned down by the police, another ten are banged up in jail. The remaining seventeen of us work here on the Project. The lads range in age from nineteen up to thirty-two.

'We started back in 1990 when the chaos after the elections made things worse for everybody. We bumped into this training guy from Solidarité who got us to see that if we continued living the way we had been we'd all pretty soon join our brothers under the soil. But if we turned over a new leaf we'd even get a piece of land, he told us. He said the guy who owned the land was so thankful for not being killed during the troubles that he had offered it to the charity as a gift.

'The rest is pretty easy, really. We fill up a 100kg plastic sack with soil and small to medium-sized stones. What we do is effectively build up a column of stone in the middle and surround it with soil. That means that it all gets roughly the same amount of water. We then cut about fifty holes in the sacks and plant sukuma wiki (a type of green cabbage) or some other green vegetable in them. One of these bags doesn't take up that much space, just about thirty centimetres by thirty centimetres. But lots of vegetables around here grow vertically. Solidarité gives us the seedlings. We have to water them twice a day, but after just four weeks you can harvest the first vegetables and then every two weeks thereafter. Obviously you don't plant them all at the same time, so you can harvest them whenever you need to.'

He tells me all of this with a calm, quiet confidence. I'm impressed and go to take a look at these sacks. Some of them already have ripe veg growing from them, others are still at the seedling stage. One of the men is picking off leaves that have gone brown and throwing them to the chickens that are running around. The chickens are also part of the Project. Anyone who works hard enough can start rearing chickens too in order to have eggs either for himself or to sell on. I come across a few hutches – they are breeding rabbits too! The rabbit hutches are built one on top of the other to maximise use of space. On top of the hutches lie clear plastic bags full of water. Six hours lying out in the hot Kenyan sun in this way is in fact a way of sterilising the water; it ensures that it is free of germs and can be used as drinking water.

Antony tells me proudly that each of them can make between €80 and €100 a month, which is enough to live on. He has a wife and two children and his wife is proud that he has honest work to do, and that the neighbours respect him. These young men have won themselves a good name. Today there are lots of people come to buy their vegetables, even occasionally a chicken. In turn they do their own bit of social work, trying to turn round other kids who are still stuck in the loop of begging, stealing and drug-taking. 'Every now and then we manage to enlist one of them in the Project,' Antony says. 'There were only twelve of us working here a year ago. Now there are seventeen.' He sits back reflectively for a moment or two and then says, 'If it weren't for Solidarité and these vegetable sacks, I'd be dead by now.' He gives me a grave look as he gets to his feet to go back to work.

I'm very impressed to see that young kids who only a year ago were drug-takers, thieves and criminals have had their lives turned round by some plastic sacks. By now there are some 70,000 households using the sacks like this, the Solidarité people tell me.

I say farewell to Antony and head off to visit a few other people. Walking along the narrow tracks that lead through the slums we have to take care not to cut ourselves on the rusty iron of the sacks. Every so often we have to jump over stinking open sewers. Everywhere you look there are people of every age and size, some of them sitting between bits of cardboard or planks of wood, trying to sell something, others hurrying along the alleyways carrying loads, usually on their heads. Almost everybody we come across glowers at us suspiciously, until we say hello and then they almost always smile back.

Anne, the quiet warrior

We're now on our way to see Anne. She's involved in the vegetable sack scheme too but lives in another part of the slum. They tell me that even here in this giant slum there are relatively 'good' and 'bad' areas. The one we're headed for now is one of the worse ones, named Soweto, after the infamous township in South Africa. To get there we make for a railway junction so that, like most of the inhabitants, we can get along faster by walking on the tracks. We're higher up now and have a better view of the entire Kibera slum, which spreads out behind the modern apartment blocks of the city centre. Local traders use the train tracks too, spreading out their wares on the sleepers. Some of them are selling shoes; others have put up little wooden stands and are selling sweets or vegetables. All around them are heaps of rubbish. Here and there little groups of people are sitting together on the tracks and chatting to one another. The railway embankment is higher up than the slum alleyways and the air is better, except that several times a day they all have to scatter when a train comes through.

After walking a fair distance along the tracks I spot some of the sacks with vegetables growing out of them down below us. To get to them we have to make our way down a steep little path. It is lucky that it is dry: when it rains this little path turns into a mudslide, making it impossible to descend. At the bottom we are greeted by a well-built lady out watering her vegetables. I put Anne's age at around sixty, but it turns out she's a decade younger, the same age as me. She's wearing a simple but clean blue-grey dress and has a cloth wrapped around her head, with a few grey hairs poking out. Anne looks after thirteen vegetable sacks placed around her little hut.

She also places some of them on the edge of the railway

track and it's clear that a lot of soil here has eroded away, which is what made the track down to her hut so steep. She shows us her sacks proudly and then invites us in. We're following Anne, who's barefoot, back down towards the little shack when all of a sudden there's a ferocious whistling and roaring noise as a huge great black train hurtles by. Anne stops at the hut, opens the door and invites us into a small dark room without windows. If she closed the door it would be pitch black, despite the sunshine outside. The room has obviously been tidied up but even so there are piles of stuff everywhere. I sit myself down on a little bench next to a small table. Anne sits down on a stool. Behind her, on top of several plastic bags, there is a black box full of gardening tools leaning against the wall.

There is a corner for cooking and on the wall is a newspaper cutting of US President Barack Obama. We're all crowded together in her nice and clean little house. It's built of wooden poles and clay, although the clay is flaking away in places. Anne reminds me of Priscilla, a woman I got to know in Mombasa years ago. I lived with her for several months in a little hut like this when I came to marry Lketinga, the story told in my first book, *The White Masai*.

I ask her a few questions and she answers me calmly in her pleasant voice. Our conversation has to compete with a rooster that calls incessantly outside and music coming from one of the other huts. I ask her how long she's lived here.

'I'm fifty years of age and I've lived in this house half my life. I come from Kisumu, a town on the western side of Kenya, Obama's side.'

I can't help laughing. I've heard that so often. Everybody from Western Kenya points out proudly that he or she comes from 'Obama's side'. Everybody, it seems, wants to claim some sort of relationship to the first black president of the USA.

'I was married young,' Anne continues, 'and had six children with my husband. Sadly two died just after birth, and so my man went off and married somebody else. His family rejected me once he had a new wife. And I couldn't go back to my own family, that's not how we do things. As soon as you're married you're part of your husband's clan. The only help my mother could offer was to get me a job as a housemaid for a family in Nairobi. So I left my children with my mother and came here to Kibera. Some friends found me this little place to live. Every day I would go into the city to clean and wash. Then a few years later my mother died and I had to bring all the kids here. There wasn't anybody else to look after them. All my other relatives were dead. So we just had to live from one day to the next, all of us crammed into this little room. The older two daughters had to look after the little ones so that I could still go to work and we just about managed to get by. There were still evenings when we went to bed hungry. I got paid a hundred shillings [about €1] a day, for washing mountains of clothing with my bare hands from dawn to dusk. On the way home I would spend thirty shillings on corn flour and the rest on charcoal, water and some fat or salt. Then there was the rent to pay. That keeps going up. When I first moved in I paid a hundred shillings a month, today it's more like six hundred. Obviously I had to walk into the city every day as I couldn't afford the bus. But if I couldn't get any washing to do, we wouldn't have had anything to eat. As it was we only managed one meal a day, and you don't sleep well if you go to bed hungry.'

I interrupt her to ask how many children still live with her, as I can't imagine living in this little room with six kids who by now must be nearly grown up. She tells me: 'The two elder girls moved out. I have no idea how they got by, because neither got married. One daughter had two children but she died when the youngest was just a year old, and so they live with me. My other daughter is dead too. I suspect both of them were HIV-positive. I couldn't afford to pay for their funerals and was happy that at least their boyfriends took care of that. My only condition was that I could be present at the funerals, so I could pay my respects. I hardly felt that I had been a good mother to them. But now I still have my four other children living here with me, so altogether that makes six children between the ages of ten and nineteen that I've got to feed.'

There's no hint of resentment in her voice, just a persistent worry. I do my sums, and soon realise that not all the children can be from her first marriage. At this she gives a hearty laugh for the first time, winks and says, 'No, I was still young and I had a boyfriend who left me with more children. He used to help me out with the rent now and then but I've no idea where he is these days. When I was still young, it could be dangerous enough living on my own here in the slums. I would get men knocking on the door, expecting to be invited in. Things were better if they knew I had a steady boyfriend. I don't need to worry so much now that I'm an old lady, but sometimes you still have to be careful when it gets dark. Some of them couldn't care less whether you're young or old. If you go out at night you never know if you might get mugged or raped. I stay home of an evening.'

I ask her if her daughter's two children are infected with HIV. She says: 'I've never had them tested as neither of them have shown any signs over the course of nine years. They say just one in four children is infected if the mother was HIV-positive, so I think my grandchildren might just be lucky.'

At that moment one of the little boys appears, gawps at us strangers, pulls on a pair of wellingtons and runs out again. I ask Anne how they all manage to sleep in such a small room, and she replies, 'Corinne, that is my biggest concern, because they're all getting bigger and need more space. The two grandchildren sleep in my bed with me. Two of the others sleep on that bench you're sitting on, sideways. But that means one of them always has his feet in the other's face. Another one of them sleeps here on the table, and another sleeps on a pile of clothes I spread on the floor when the door is closed. We have to all eat together first because there's no room to move when we're all lying down. In the mornings I get up early, and get the children out to school. Unfortunately I can't give them anything to eat to take with them, because I can't afford it. They have to see what they can find along the way.'

All this time the radio next door is still blaring and the rooster's still crowing his head off.

'But life has got a lot better for us since I've had these vegetable sacks from Solidarité,' she adds with a smile. 'It means we at least always have something to eat every day. I can either cook my own vegetables or sell a few bunches. I make about thirty shillings a week like that. Life isn't bad. Every day we have ugali [a maize dish eaten like porridge or made thicker into dumplings] with kale. If we don't have much money we just make the ugali thinner so it's more like a soup. The only thing is you can't keep it long. But the thirteen vegetable sacks guarantee us at least one meal a day. Then a couple of days a week I do washing for other people, so we can pay the rent. Otherwise the landlord would be round to take away the door or even the roof over our heads until we've paid up. If that happens and the rains come, you can lose everything. Even with a roof, you still get water pouring in, and it's still cold at night.'

I find myself dumbstruck, amazed how Anne does whatever she can to feed her children and grandchildren, while refusing to complain about her lot. She seems proud that she's managed to up their standard of living after two years of hard work cultivating the veggie bags.

Before I leave, I ask her is she has any dreams for her future. 'Yes,' she says, 'the one thing I wish for is a house of my own, even if it's just a little place, no bigger than this. But it has to be mine, so that my children can be sure of having a roof over their heads after I die. As things stand every day I worry the landlord is going to turn up and demand his house back. Despite the fact we've lived here so long and everybody is so jammed together, I still don't know my neighbours well. I don't even know what they do for a living. Maybe one of them's a night watchman, maybe one of them works for a bank, and maybe they don't do anything at all. Nobody here really mixes with anybody else. Everyone is just out for themselves.'

There's no way I can leave without giving her some money so that at least she has enough to pay the next month's rent and doesn't have to worry about this evening's meal. I can see from her face that she wasn't expecting it and is absolutely delighted. She takes me by the hand and gives me such an intense look of gratitude that it bring tears to my eyes.

We go back out into the blinding sunshine. There's clean laundry hanging on a line, fluttering in the wind above the filthy ground. We set off to find the next soul willing to share their life story with us. I turn round one last time to see Anne standing barefoot outside her little hut, waving us a fond farewell.

Cabbage instead of rat poison – how Irene's life was saved

We're off to see Irene, just twenty-three years old, HIV-positive and single mother of two, or so Pastor Elly, who's taking us to meet her, tells me. On our way we pass a stall selling leftover bits of fish: fish heads or skeletons with the heads and tails still attached laid out to dry in the sun, covered in flies. Pastor Elly tells me that in the evening the dried remains are boiled up to make fish soup. He does what he can with modest means – sometimes no more than a few kind words – to minister to a flock of three thousand households, some of which are extremely poor indeed.

Children keep running up to say hello. They nearly all say the same thing: 'How are you? How are you?' Some of the tin shacks here are painted in gaudy colours. One of them, just in front of us, is painted blue with pictures of all sorts of exotic hairstyles. But the door to what is obviously the local hair-dresser's is closed. It would seem there are no more customers expected today. A few steps further on we come across a rose bush planted next to a tin wall. It is an unexpectedly fragrant and colourful natural wonder in these intensely unfamiliar surroundings.

Certain aspects of the slum are both fascinating and repellent. You continually come across situations that for most

Europeans are completely alien, but that doesn't mean it's all misery and tragedy. It just depends on the people. People laugh, debate, sometimes argue, but the children for the most part seem happy, even if some of them look older than their years. The alleys and footpaths might be dirty and grimy but by and large people keep their clothes clean, which astonishes me as after just a few hours in Kibera I'm filthy from head to foot.

One woman is selling mandazi. I love these little triangular doughnuts. She has set up a plastic bowl full of them on a little stool. The man on her left is selling tin cans full of charcoal, while the man on her right has made a machine to sharpen knives from bits of a bicycle.

Pastor Elly stops when we come up to this woman and introduces her to us as Irene. I hold out my hand to her. She looks a lot older than twenty-three, even though I can see she's wearing what clearly used to be a school uniform underneath her green dress. She has a baby on one hip but looks gaunt and lean. She has her hair plaited in tight rows along her skull and differently coloured flip-flops on her feet.

She takes us over to her hut, which unlike Anne's is made completely of corrugated iron. She's covered the walls inside with cloth hangings to make it seem just a little more homely and there's a sheet of thick plastic on the floor. No window here either. We sit ourselves down on a little bench and she perches on the end of her narrow bed. Behind her is a big sheet of prettily embroidered cloth designed to hide her bed somewhat. She puts the child, who is about nine months old, down in a little plastic chair, gives it a lollipop and starts telling us about herself, mentioning in the first sentence that if it weren't for Solidarité and Pastor Elly, she'd be dead.

I want to hear her story from the beginning and start by asking her how long she's been living in the slums. She speaks in a quiet voice, not least so that the neighbours won't hear as every word penetrates the thin walls.

'I came here back in 2003, when I was sixteen. Before that

I lived in Western Kenya. We lived on a small farm and I was the oldest of nine children. My dad was a bus driver for the school that my best friend and I went to. She was a bit older than me. Life was pretty good really, until my mother died, just after I'd finished fourth form. I don't know what she died of. But when I think back on it now, I think she just died of grief, because after her funeral I found out that my father had been having an affair with my best friend. It was a shock to me and I believe that was what killed my mother. As the oldest child, it was now up to me to look after the farm and my little brothers and sisters, so I had to give up school.

'It got worse. My dad married the girl who had been my schoolmate. One minute she was my best friend, the next she was my stepmother. It was impossible for me to see her with my father so soon after the death of my mother. It turned into hell – we turned into bitter enemies. She treated me badly and tried to dump all the domestic work on me. She kept going on at me to find a boyfriend of my own, as at sixteen years of age I was too old to continue to live with them. Eventually I couldn't take it any more and went off to live with an aunt in Kisumu. But I couldn't get on there either as she and her husband argued all the time. She suggested I go to Nairobi to get a job as a housemaid. She said she knew somebody in Kimera who could help me. And she really did: she found me a job as a maid to a really nice woman. I got fed and paid, the work wasn't too hard and the woman was nice to me. But a few months later she had to go off to Mombasa for some reason and didn't know when she'd be coming back. She said I should go back to the farm and she'd call to let me know when she needed me again. So once again I had no job and no money.'

Irene told me her life story without expression, without anger, just quietly and almost as if she was on automatic pilot. 'I went back to my father but it wasn't going to work. He didn't want me back home any more. My aunt in Kisumu had separated from her husband but she'd got a new boyfriend, and I had simply no idea who to turn to, what to do. Then one day

I met a guy I had known since I was in the second form at school. We were good friends but we'd never slept together. He said I could stay with him, but before long we ended up having sex and I got pregnant almost straight away. He didn't want any responsibility for it and so we split up. For a second time I headed off to my aunt's friend in Kibera, this time heavily pregnant. She said I could stay until the child was born. She told her work colleagues about me and after my little daughter was born they let me take her to a kindergarten. The boss was a friend of my aunt's friend and didn't charge me for looking after the baby. In fact, she was good enough to find this place for me to live and even paid three months' rent in advance to give me enough time to find work.

'At first I had no furniture at all, not even this piece of plastic on the floor, just a few pieces of newspaper and cardboard, and when it rained the water came in. But I didn't need to cook because when I went to pick up my baby in the evening they gave me a meal. For a while at least, my life wasn't too bad. But then everything went to pieces, particularly here in the slums after the riots that followed the 2007 elections. I went out every day looking for work: cleaning, doing washing, anything at all just to make enough money to get by. But it got harder and harder: I'm from the Luo tribe and in those days no Kikuyu would offer us a job. There was next to no food to be had. So when a man offered to marry me and look after me and the baby I was really happy, even though I had promised never again to let myself be used by some man. He was a bit older, though, and seemed to be a serious type, so I trusted him, especially when he promised to do something for my brothers and sisters back home. We're both Catholics though and as the Church doesn't allow condoms or any other forms of contraceptive I was soon pregnant again. When it was getting near my time, I went to the closest hospital, which was in a tent. Like all other mothers in Kenya I had to have a blood test and found out, just a few hours before my second child was due to be born, that I was HIV-positive. My blood count was high, though, which indicated I had only recently been infected. It was terrible news to hear just before I was about to give birth. Immediately I was transferred to another hospital tent that made a point of doing everything possible to make sure the infection wasn't passed on to the baby. My hospital fees were taken care of because of this, but it wasn't much compensation. I was just twenty-two years old and had already been sentenced to death.

'Back home I told my husband he'd given me the AIDS virus and told him he should go to the doctor so he could get treated too. But all he did was get angry and tell me I'd got it the wrong way round: I must have given him the virus. It wasn't his baby. I should just clear off out of there. He didn't want anything more to do with me.'

When she mentioned her infection, Irene's voice dropped to a whisper. Nobody in the neighbourhood knew, it appeared, and if they did, they wouldn't have anything to do with her. She was terrified of being treated like a leper. Once a week she went to the clinic to get her medicine and took a long detour on the way to make sure nobody spotted her.

Her little daughter all this time is sucking on a lollipop and is a complete sticky mess, not that anybody minds. Outside somebody is making a frightful din working with some piece of metal. Irene seems used to it. She just continues with her story as if nothing is going on. 'After that man threw me out I decided never to get married again. I was still only young but already had two children and now this disease. In our culture there's no shame in not being married. But I was desperate too and couldn't see how I was going to get by. I had no food and I couldn't even work as the child was still a tiny baby. I moved back into this hut with no furniture and the rent to find.

'I lost the will to live. I used my last few shillings to buy rat poison, laid down on the bare ground with my baby at my breast and let the events of my short life run through my mind. I was freezing too: it gets very cold at night in these tin huts. I just couldn't see why it had all gone so wrong, when so many of my schoolfriends had done well. Why didn't I finish school? Why had I had so much bad luck? Why did life punish me so much? Why was everything so unfair? As I thought through it all, I started praying and continued praying half the night. And gradually the idea of taking my own life faded. Apart from anything else I remembered that to do so would be a sin in the eyes of God. Instead I decided I would let God decide when my time had come. It didn't seem like it would be that far away anyhow. For the next few days I just sat here in the hut waiting to see what would happen. Eventually somebody knocked on the door. I was hardly able to get to my feet to open the door. There was a woman outside asking if she could do anything to help. She said she was from the Church. I could hardly believe it. She promised straight away to bring me a bed and something to eat. At least my baby and I would no longer have to sleep on the ground. I hadn't seen the older girl, who was two by now, for ages. I simply hadn't had the energy to go and pick her up from the kindergarten.

'I was convinced that God had answered my prayers and from that day on my faith was stronger than ever. At night I would lie on my bed and pray, "Dear God, show me what I must do with my life. Give me the strength that my children and I might survive." But all the time I was still getting thinner because I had so little to eat but still had to breastfeed the baby. Eventually the day came when I could no longer go on, but then a miracle happened: Pastor Elly came to me.'

At this point Pastor Elly himself joins in. 'When I first came across Irene with her newborn child, I thought this woman is dying, she was so thin. She was little more than skin and bones. I came to see her several times, brought her food and told her about Solidarité and how they organised growing your own food in sacks.'

An aircraft drones overhead, drowning out even the noise of the metal beating outside. The little girl wants her mummy. Irene picks her up, sits her on her lap and continues:

'Yes, when Pastor Elly came to me it was the second time

God had reached out his hand to me. God had heard my prayers and once again he had sent someone. I was so grateful I listened to every word Pastor Elly said. He told me about these Solidarité people and their sack gardens. He told me that if I signed up he would help me to plant the first bag, because he could see that I was still too weak to fill a hundred-kilogram sack with stones and earth on my own. The Solidarité people even waived the purchase price of the sack because I was so poor and weak. Normally you have to buy the sack and find the soil to fill it. You have to show you are willing to make an effort, then they give you the seedlings and instructions on how to grow them. Pastor Elly promised me that I would soon be able to grow my own vegetables so I said I would work at it as hard as I was able. I also found a place in the church community, got to know more people and for the first time I was able to talk about my illness and no longer felt so isolated.'

I ask Irene how much her life has changed. Her face immediately brightens and she gives a laugh. 'Hey, my life has changed totally. I have a garden. I make two to three hundred shillings a week and have more than enough vegetables to eat. I even managed to save a bit and started up the mandazi business. Every morning I get up at five to bake the mandazi, then I sell them, and afterwards work on my sack garden.

I ask how much rent she pays and am amazed to hear she pays a thousand shillings, nearly €10. Irene is surprised in turn that I am so shocked and says: 'Corinne, when I was so thin and ill, my child nearly died. It was so cold in here we shivered all night. The doctors at the clinic said that unless I could keep my child a bit warmer she wouldn't survive. My landlord took pity on me and installed electricity free. Now I have a light bulb and that provides just a little bit of heat too. But that's why I have to pay nearly double the normal rent.'

I find it hard to believe that a single light bulb can provide any heat, but then Pastor Elly tells me it's a special bulb, used to help chicken eggs hatch, and gives out more warmth than normal.

To me, Irene still looks so frail that I can hardly believe she manages to tend all her veggie sacks on her own. But she says she's recovered so well over the past nine months that she manages it quite easily. Her will to live astonishes me.

Later, when she's showing us her garden, Irene says she's going to have to replace some of the sacks as the heat outdoors means they don't last much more than a year or so. She doesn't keep it as tidy as Anne. There are bits of paper and other debris lying between some of the white sacks. But she stands there proudly, showing off the green veg growing out of them.

Before we take our leave I ask Irene if she's content with her lot. 'Oh yes,' she says with a much stronger voice than she used when she was starting out on her story, 'I'm very happy. I've forgiven the man who infected me. I'm dreaming of going back to school and getting an education. Maybe I'll manage to find some evening classes and learn how to do something that makes more money.'

Yet again, I find myself amazed at the hand fate deals out to some people. This young woman is still striving to better herself, despite the relatively meagre existence she leads. She's not even dreaming of a nicer house, a television or some other material goods: she's dreaming of an education.

Doreen's indomitable survival instinct

By now it's become really hot and our tummies are rumbling. The woman from Solidarité knows a place here in the Kibera slum where we can get something to eat before we go on to our final visit. It's a simple but clean little snack room that serves only traditional African food. I'm delighted. At last a proper African meal eaten the proper African way: with our fingers. We're the only white people present and draw a lot of attention. I trust the food and it tastes delicious. When I leave Nairobi, I will look back on it as the best meal I had, served in the country's biggest slum!

Fed and watered, we set off on our way to the last inter-viewee, who lives in yet another part of the slum, called

Gatwekera. Our feet are sweating in our wellington boots as we plod along the alleyways amid crowds of children smiling and waving at us, none of them in school uniform. Some of them are just sitting and playing on the bare ground. Lots of them seem to have colds and their noses are either dripping or bunged up. There are far more of them running around everywhere than there were earlier so I guess school must be over for the day.

We pass a man sitting on a cardboard box under an umbrella repairing other brollies and shoes. His legs are stretched out in front of him, his feet in socks full of holes. But he seems happy enough. Everywhere you look it's the same picture: everybody doing whatever they can to earn a few shillings. Here there's somebody mending something, over there is somebody sharpening knives, and there's somebody selling stuff. It's hardly right to say everybody here just sits around and does nothing.

We get back to the train tracks and this time walk in the opposite direction. Here too there are lots more people than there were earlier. After walking for about twenty minutes we climb up over the embankment and leave the tracks behind us. I can see the white sacks already in the distance, all laid out in orderly rows, veg hanging out of them. And there isn't a heap of junk to be seen nearby. There's nobody working on them at present, as it's still lunchtime, and in any case it's far too hot.

I have to be careful not to fall into several ditches filled with filthy water on the way. We take a left turn, then a right and all of a sudden I'm not sure where we are any more. All I can see is an endless vista of tin huts, a heap of garbage with a brown chicken on top of it, laying an egg as we pass. Every step we take is watched by dozens of children, and there are washing lines everywhere with colourful children's clothing hanging on them.

We come across a narrow little path flanked by mud huts behind a drainage ditch full of dirty water. The pastor stops at an open door and shouts inside. Then a large, stocky woman with two children in her arms appears and asks us inside. She introduces herself as Doreen. The room is bigger than either Anne's or Irene's and has got colourful flowery carpets on the ground and clothing hanging from wires running round the walls. There's a crocheted tablecloth on the table and in the middle of it a mobile phone, albeit a very basic one. How crazy is that? I ask myself when people here have barely enough to live on. But here we even have proper wooden armchairs to sit on. One of the kids looks at me, this big white woman, and suddenly bursts into tears. It's the first time in hours that I've actually heard a child here cry. It something I remember from before: in Africa there are kids everywhere but you rarely hear them crying. A neighbour comes in and takes the crying child out.

Doreen is very different to either Anne or Irene. An attractive woman, she seems very self-confident and bursting with strength. She is forty-two years old, HIV-positive and a widow. She has given birth to seven children. She has striking high cheekbones and her eyes sparkle as she tells me her story. Her hair is cut short and is already grey at the temples. She has a sensual mouth and knows the impression she makes. She doesn't look at all sick, which is obviously because she is taking anti-AIDS drugs. She comes from Bondo, near Lake Victoria. She got married young and had her first child, a girl, at the age of seventeen. She has a strong, clear voice and when she gets angry you'd think she was spoiling for a fight.

She arrived in Nairobi's Kibera slum back in 2004. She tells me how it happened. 'After my husband died in February of 2004 I didn't know what to do, where to go. We had lived in his village since we got married and I'd had six children by him. Then suddenly, when our youngest was just two years old, he took ill. He continued to deteriorate and I took him to hospital. That was when I found out he had AIDS. They tested me too and diagnosed that I was also HIV-positive. A few months later he died and I had to bring his body back home to be buried. That cost a lot of money and I was left with next to nothing.

'His family refused to help me or the children. This was partly because of my infection but partly just because with my husband dead my link to their clan was gone. I couldn't go back to my own family because both my parents were dead and all my sisters were married into other families. I had nobody to belong to. That was when I realised my old life was simply over, gone, and I had to start a new life. The family gave me three months to sort myself out.'

As long as I've been in Kenya, I keep hearing the same story from different women. Even back in the days when I lived among the Samburu it was the custom that as soon as a girl got married she belonged to her husband's clan. Sometimes she wasn't even allowed to see her own family again. I was shocked at first and put it down to an old Samburu nomadic tradition. And then there was the fact that they lived in the wilderness with no means of communication or transport. But I've since come to realise that it's the same everywhere you go in Kenya. I can't help thinking that without the women, the whole country would go to pot, yet time and time again it's the women who lose out.

Doreen continues her story. 'At the end of the three months I set off for Nairobi because I had heard I could get a job here washing and cleaning. I ended up in Kibera and met my second husband in a pub. He lived here in this house. I told him I was HIV before I brought all my children here with me. But he didn't believe it and said he loved me anyway and wanted me to come and live with him. I looked fit and well so there was no way I could be sick and anyway he didn't really believe the AIDS virus existed. He simply didn't want to know. So that's how I ended up here in this house. Before long I was pregnant again, but I lost the baby.

'Obviously we were all a bit cramped living here in one room. As time went on I would see less and less of my husband. Meanwhile I kept hearing that one or another of his old girlfriends had died. I mentioned it to him and asked him to get tested for AIDS so he could get medicine. But he refused even to talk about it. Shortly after he took ill himself. But even then he wouldn't go to hospital or take any medicine. Only two years after burying my first husband, the second one died too, in February 2006. Now it was hard for me to get enough to feed us all and pay the two thousand shillings a month rent. My eldest daughter got married and moved out. She's twenty-five now. I couldn't make enough money doing washing for other people so I started making changa, the local beer.'

That took me straight back to Barsaloi, where my mother-in-law also used to brew this beer. It was a foul-tasting brown liquid, but it was strong and cheap. She would always get drunk easily and become rather merry. I have to smile at this part of Doreen's story.

'So I would sell beer and make good money out of it. I would hide the bottles under the bed because it's illegal. It's against the law to make this sort of beer in Kenya and even more so to sell it. But I had no choice. We needed food and money for the older children so they could go to school. My customers would come here to drink. That could be dangerous. One day I realised that my children were becoming too acquainted with alcohol. Even when I wasn't here customers would come and my ten-year-old daughter would sell them beer. I worried that maybe the police would come and arrest the children. My instinct as a mother told me I had to give it up.

'During this time, however, I got to know another man. He moved in, did a bit of work from time to time and would support me. I told him I had AIDS but he didn't believe me either because I looked so healthy. Obviously I was pleased to have a man supporting me not least because a woman on her own in the slum is likely to be robbed.'

I can't get over the attitude of the men here and it's starting to make me angry. But it seems to be the case that the men don't worry about the dangers of infection and just live their lives as if there's no such thing. But then, when I look at

Doreen, I can't believe she's carrying this deadly virus either. And there's something about her that fascinates me. She's so jolly, so full of life, and it makes me feel good to be in her company. When she's talking she waves her arms all over the place, quite the opposite of Irene, who just sat there with her hands in her lap.

Doreen is talking again. 'I got pregnant by this man too.' She points to the little girl sitting on her knee. 'I saved up money for the clinic to try to make sure that my daughter didn't catch the virus. But it didn't work out. When I went into labour I set off with my neighbour on the long journey to the hospital. But we only got so far when my waters broke and I realised I was about to give birth. I had no choice but to bring my daughter into the world lying on the pavement. My neighbour helped me. Then I had to decide whether to take the newborn child on to the hospital or just to go home with her. Back home I had hungry children who could do with the money being spent on food for them. And in any case I had nothing to wrap the newborn up in. I felt dirty and weak, and in the end I just turned round and came home, with the result that my youngest daughter is infected too.'

For the first time Doreen's voice goes quiet. It occurs to me too that the right thing to have done would have been to carry on to the hospital. On the other hand, I can't imagine how a woman of over forty years of age who's just given birth on the pavement could be expected to trudge several kilometres on foot to a hospital. Back in Switzerland she'd have been in a clean hospital bed, looked after and taken care of. Most women are exhausted after giving birth and need to rest for several days.

In Doreen's case it was different. She came back home, and the children cooked dinner so she could have a bit of a rest. 'When you're really in trouble,' she tells me, 'heaven always sends somebody or something to help. In this case it was a good thing that the baby came on a Friday. It meant I could rest over the weekend. My children looked after me and my boyfriend cooked. By Monday I was ready again to take over my duties in the kitchen and the next week I was able to start taking in washing again. Obviously it's hard on your back when you have to bend over all day washing dirty clothes by hand, but I'm just grateful there are still jobs like this to be had because so few people in the city have washing machines.

'Not long after I gave birth, however, chaos broke out and things started to go wrong again in my life. One day my boy-friend simply didn't come back. I still have no idea where he might be or even if he's still alive. All of a sudden there were no jobs any more and people were fighting and there was blood flowing. Nobody trusted anybody else any more. That was when I first heard about Solidarité. I heard that there was this charity organisation handing out food vouchers in another part of the slum. We had been starving for days, so I went along.

'There was a huge queue of people waiting. When I finally got to the front the woman there told me I wasn't entitled to a food ticket because I wasn't local. I could hardly believe she could turn me and my hungry children down. We could have used the vouchers to go and buy six kilos of maize meal in the shops, as well as lard and other essentials. I came home realising there was nothing left for me to do but beg. But a few days later it was the turn of our part of the slum to get the vouchers, and this time they gave me some. I enjoyed the fact that the woman who handed them to me was the same woman who had turned me down a couple of days earlier.

'Well, that was my first encounter with Solidarité. I still had no idea about these so-called "sack gardens". It was only a couple of weeks later that a man came and told me about them. He invited me to come along to one of their weekly meetings to hear more. The whole project seemed great to me and I used the money I got the next time I took washing in to buy some empty sacks and began filling them up with rocks and soil. When I had done all that, they gave me the seedlings. Since then my life has been transformed. Before, when I had no work, I would just sit here at home, even though I wanted to work. There just weren't enough jobs. Now, I still take in washing, but on top of that I have a guaranteed source of income. I have enough veg for the family and I can sell the rest for three hundred shillings a week. And because I've worked so hard at it, I've now been allowed to join the "chicken project", which means we also have eggs and chicken to eat.'

To make the point, Doreen pulls out a washing-up bowl from under her bed with a chicken in it sitting on several eggs. It's such a surprise that we all burst out laughing.

The woman from Solidarité adds: 'We give the hard workers six chickens and a cockerel so they can start breeding their own.' She asks Doreen where the other chickens are. She looks a bit embarrassed by this. 'Ah, I did something a bit silly over Christmas. I was really keen to give my children a special meal for once, and decided to kill one of my chickens because to buy one would have cost a thousand shillings, which is the equivalent of half a month's rent. I thought I'd soon have another one to replace her, but then I realised that instead of one of the chickens it was the cockerel whose neck I had wrung.' We all burst out laughing again. Doreen has a way of telling stories. But I'm shocked simply to hear that a chicken costs the equivalent of €10 when I think of how cheaply, thanks to the subsidies paid to chicken farmers, we can buy them in Europe.

'But the upside is,' Doreen adds, 'that the children had a great Christmas dinner.'

Outside I can hear her neighbours chattering and a baby crying, and the roar of an aircraft engine; the airport is not far. Before we leave I ask Doreen if her neighbours and children know about her infection. To my surprise she answers loudly and almost jovially, 'Oh yes, I talk to people about it all the time. It would be too much stress not to. I'm a realist: you have to play the hand life deals you. Lots of people act as if there was nothing wrong with them, but I think you just have to face up to it. If one of my neighbours offers me a Coke or a beer, I ask them if I could have some milk instead because it's better for me. If you have to take medicines regularly then you have to stick to a simple diet. My children know all about it too. There's no point in pretending. I just tell them they all have to work hard at school so they can help one another out when I'm no longer around. They know they have to pay attention in school. That's just the way I am. Doreen's way, I call it.

'But as long as Solidarité is around, I think there's no limit to what I can do. I can plant more sacks, get more chickens, and maybe go on to stage three soon: keeping rabbits. The only trouble is there's not much room here in the slums. That's why my dream is that one day I can afford to buy a little patch of land that my children can call home.'

We take our leave of Doreen and, as I did with the other people we've been to see, I hand her a month's rent. For me it's not a big deal, but for her it's the equivalent of being paid for taking in twenty loads of washing. When I meet women like these and hear about the conditions they have to live in, and their modest dreams, I feel really small and ashamed of those days in my affluent life when I grumble about things.

When we come back to Nairobi five months later, Klaus and I go back to find the vegetable sack ladies. Once again Pastor Elly and some of the women from Solidarité come with us. By the time we get to Doreen's hut, yet again having to jump over ditches filled with sewage and dirty water, it seems to me as if Kibera is even filthier and stinks more than it did last time.

In the meantime things have changed for the better for Doreen, she tells us with a broad smile. She's been on a course to learn how to look after newborn children, the chronically ill and how to improve hygiene conditions in the slums. She's now teaching everybody else what's she's learnt. That gives her a lot of pleasure but the absolute best thing in her life is that she has finally fulfilled her dream of giving her children a roof of their own over their heads. She's bought a tiny piece of land back home in what she calls 'Obama's area'. Now she's doing all she can to save enough money to build a little house there. It's not easy, she says, because she still has to find the money to pay for her brightest boy to go to secondary school.

'But things have gone so well for me over the past few months that I feel certain God will help me once again,' she says humbly.

By contrast I'm shocked when we go back to see Irene. She's even thinner than before and her school uniform skirt barely rests on her hips. She has weeping spots all over her arms and face, and even those that have healed up have left scars. She says her HIV infection has all but destroyed her immune system and she nearly died. 'But as you can see, I managed to get through it. Take a look at my new business,' she says, pointing to some corn cobs on a barbecue. With a grin she asks if we want to buy some, for 1 shilling [1 cent] each. The best we'll get anywhere, she boasts.

We go back also to see Anne, who as ever is busy tending her veggie sack garden. She gives us big warm smile and invites us into her hut. There hasn't been much change in her life since we were last here.

What I find most touching in my encounters with all these women is how delighted they are to see us so interested in their lives. It's Anne who expresses it best, bringing tears to my eyes. 'I didn't have a visitor in years until you turned up to see me last February, and I haven't had one since. I'm overjoyed to welcome you back again to my little home. You gave me such encouragement to carry on, despite all life's difficulties. It was just so inspiring to know that there are people living outside the slums who might care about me and my life. You filled me with a sense of self-respect.'

JAMII BORA

A song and dance is not the usual greeting you get in a bank back home in Switzerland, but it's standard in Kenya whenever you come into contact with the Jamii Bora credit union. Whether it's in the bank buildings, somebody's office or one of the projects they lend money to, guests are welcomed with singing and hand clapping. I can't help thinking we should try it back in Europe. I'm sure it would do wonders for business.

We're in the car park on our way to the main entrance of Jamii Bora's head office when we're greeted by six women singing and clapping, who run ahead to show us the way to the building. My mind is still reeling from the welcome as we go inside to find ourselves in a large hall with all sorts of tables and counters, and people patiently waiting their turn. There's someone over in one corner filling out forms; in another corner someone else is deep in discussion. It all seems very calm and businesslike, with all the customers clearly content. The vast majority of them are women.

A tubby elderly woman introduces herself as Susanne and says she's in charge. She sets about explaining the history of the business before introducing us to Ingrid, the founder, and some of the organisation's biggest customers. She says she has rags-to-riches stories to tell us that you can only otherwise hear in the USA, about bottle-washers who've ended up millionaires.

'This project began back in 1993, among a group of women beggars,' she tells us, but her words only whet our appetites as she says the founder will want to tell us the story for herself. But she is happy to tell us how it all works.

'This branch has been open just since 2007 and already has 12,000 members. Throughout Kenya in total there are more than 260,000 members, whether savers or borrowers. The system is very simple: you need five people who agree to act as guarantors for one another. Once they've got themselves together, they can register. Two weeks later each of them gets a card with all their data on it, including their fingerprint to guard against fraud. This card is absolutely essential. From the moment they get it, they can start saving. The minimal contribution is 50 shillings [€0.50] a week. After they have saved regularly for six weeks, they are entitled to borrow up to double the amount in their account. There is interest to be paid of course, but the rate is much lower than you'd get from a bank. Initially the cut-off figure is 10,000 shillings [€100]. If you have saved that much you can borrow 20,000 shillings [€200]. Then, if you pay that back, you can ask to borrow 40,000 shillings [€400] next time, and so on. There is also insurance cover provided in case of an accident or illness, which includes paying the hospital bills. Husbands have to take out insurance of their own, which costs more. Nearly all the borrowers are women with children.' Susanne adds that Ingrid will answer any other questions we might have.

But now the women have all started chanting again, singing the praises of Jamii Bora as they accompany us up the stairs to talk to some of the customers who've made good with the money they borrowed while we wait to speak to Ingrid, whom they all call 'Mama'.

We go into a room where there are two young men and a slightly older woman seated at a huge desk. I'm not too impressed with the men, who look bored, but the woman is captivating. She is sitting there with a white headscarf framing a face that to me seems both marked with wisdom and good-ness. Everything about her is totally African. She gives her name as Joyce, and starts to tell us her story.

Joyce's story – from a single mother on the streets to a successful businesswoman

'Originally I come from a rural district in the Rift Valley. My husband and I had a little house on a hectare of land, with cows, goats, sheep and chickens. Life was hard but it was good. We had five children: three girls and two boys. But then in 1992 the time of troubles began. We're Kikuyu and back then everybody was at war with us. For weeks on end people robbed, stole, raped women and children and burnt down homes.

'Everything was in chaos. I grabbed my kids in a fit of panic and somehow or other made my way to Nairobi. I lost my husband in all the commotion. It was the same for lots of people. Some seven thousand people died and another two hundred and fifty thousand fled their homes.

'At first the children and I lived on the streets, subsisting from hand to mouth. We knew nobody and had to beg for a living. But God was good to me. After a while I ran into Elizabeth who had also fled from our village. She was working in a forestry plantation and had a big room and could offer us somewhere to live. I tried for a job too as a farmer's daughter and Elizabeth got me a hoe and a sickle, what we call a panga. For the next few months I worked in the forest and bushland and must have cleared a hectare on my own,' she says with a modest smile.

'When the work there was done, I tried to see what else I could do. I did what lots of other people did: went from door to door looking for washing to do, though as I'm a fast, good worker, I could ask for more money than most of them. By the end of the week I'd earned 9,000 shillings [€90] and also got to know lots of people. They all kept telling me I should go into a government office and beg until they gave me a little piece of land to work so I could build up something for myself. So I did what they said and kept at them again and again and again until God had mercy on me and I got a tiny piece of land, just seventy metres by seventy but with some wood and tin as well, enough for me and the kids to build ourselves a little house with two rooms. We were very pleased with ourselves and I would have loved to have shown it off to my husband, if I'd had any idea what had happened to him. Kenya's so big that it's impossible to find somebody if you don't know where to look.'

That reminded me of my own story. I know just how hard it is to find somebody in Kenya. Back then I scoured half of Kenya to find my great love, the Samburu warrior Lketinga, equipped with only a few photos of him. For days on end I travelled back and forth across the country until I ended up in Maralal in the Samburu country, which was more or less the end of the road. I spent days there wandering around showing his picture to people who could hardly understand me and asking them if they had any idea where I might find this man. If it hadn't been for the will of God, and a lot of luck, my life would have been totally different and I can't help but think I would never have had my beautiful daughter.

But all this time, Joyce is still telling her story: 'I made a living by washing clothes until one day I heard about Jamii Bora. I was curious and found out all about it. I was told I had to save 50 shillings a week and make sure I fulfilled all the criteria necessary to become a customer. I did the best I could and within eighteen months I had saved 3,500 shillings [€35] and was able to borrow twice that sum. Me and my children got together and tried to decide what to do with the money to make more. They are more educated than me. I only attended school for a few years but I'm clever enough,' she says, laughing.

'We decided to use one room of our house as a tearoom. That meant we all had to sleep in one room but we didn't mind. I used the money to have two tables and four benches made. I bought tea, milk and sugar, as well as lard and maize flour to make chapattis. We started out very modestly offering just tea and ugali, our local maize dish, and the chapattis. But word soon got around that this Kikuyu woman Joyce could cook well and ran a nice clean place. I went out into the slums and offered the food I cooked to the schools. Before long I had a contract with four primary schools. But I didn't have enough money for that at first, and so I took out some more credit, 20,000 shillings [€200] this time.

'Business went well. Anyone who had a bit of money bought either ugali or a chapatti. After a few months I was selling so much I couldn't carry it on the bus any more, so I decided to buy a second-hand car. I sent one of my sons to learn to drive and saved hard so that within a few months I could borrow up to 10,000 shillings [€100], which meant we could easily afford a car.'

Every time it comes to money I have to tell myself that 1,000 Kenyan shillings is just €10. Buying a car for €100 seems very cheap to me, but I know that for somebody like Joyce it's a huge amount of money. I keep having to tell myself to take two zeroes off the end of every sum she mentions so I can see how much it is in euros.

'By now things were really doing well,' Joyce goes on. 'We were running three little restaurants. The children were older too and those who were nearly grown up could help out. Not only that, but I was able to hire a few people. We all worked really hard and our dreams were coming true. Thanks to the Jamii Bora system we could really build up the business. But I needed to invest the money or it would depreciate, so we began buying up little plots of land and had simple little huts built on them and rented them out. I'd become a landlord!' she beams proudly.

'Corinne,' she says, 'don't forget that just a couple of years earlier I had nothing. I'd lost my husband and was living out on the streets with five children. When summer came and it began to get really hot in Nairobi, I branched out and started offering fresh fruit juices, which turned out to be really popular. The main restaurant was doing well and if it had been larger I could have done even better. I thought long and hard about it and in the end decided to rip it all down and put up a new building with three floors. I couldn't do the design myself, but my educated children, the youngest son in particular, helped me. I went back to Jamii Bora with these new plans and had a chat with Ingrid. This time I wanted to borrow 1.5 million shillings [€15,000]. Such a lot of money, just think of it, Corinne. But I was sure it would all work out and I'd be able to pay it all back. I'm intelligent and a hard worker still, even if I was getting older. I got the loan, but then when we had built the new restaurant I found I needed another half a million shillings to fit it out.

'At the same time I was starting to breed chickens. That was a business I'd known since childhood. It only takes six weeks before the chickens are old enough to be slaughtered and eaten or sold on. What I did was to add them to the menu. The money just poured in so before long I had enough to do a proper new fit-out. And all this time I was still selling my meals on the contract with the schools.

'Then things went horribly wrong. One morning in May 2007, around five in the morning, my brand new three-storey restaurant, all built of wood, caught fire and burned to the ground. It was no accident, it was arson. I was horrified. Straight away I went to Ingrid, who called in the police and a loss adjustment man from the insurance company. But I was still left 70,000 shillings out of pocket.

'I wasn't going to give up though. I went back to Jamii Bora yet again and told them this time I needed to borrow two million shillings so I could rebuild the restaurant, out of stone this time so it couldn't burn down. They gave me it, and 100,000 on top, the biggest loan they had ever made. And now I'm almost ready to reopen the new restaurant. Think of that!' she finishes with a beaming smile.

This woman sitting there so calmly, straight-backed on her chair in front of me, has a lot to be proud of. She refused to give up, and, despite her lack of education, has turned herself into a proper businesswoman in just a few years.

Just to round things off, she tells me jubilantly: 'We're not born to be poor, you see. That's not what God wants. I'm proof that anybody can be successful. I lost everything at one stage, but with hard work and determination, I won out and today I have sixty-two employees, seven houses and I have to admit that over the past seven years, I've actually become rich. And even though I'm sixty-four years old, I still have big plans. God bless Ingrid and the good work she does, and may God give her the strength to keep going and help more and more people from the slums, by lending them money when the big banks wouldn't even let them through the door.'

Yet again I find myself deeply moved by her story: her will to survive, her courage and self-confidence amazes me. She is, quite simply, a remarkable woman. All the time I've been listening to her, I've been impressed by the strength of character and energy she exudes. She may be sixty-four, but she's not thinking of retiring any time soon.

Before we leave I ask if she ever heard any more from her husband. She grins and says, 'Yes. We've been back together since 1999. We met by some miracle of chance in Nairobi. A year later I borrowed some more money and we held a big party to celebrate the renewal of our marriage. He's seventy-six now but I'm happy to support him because, after all, he's the father of my children.' Then she laughs and adds: 'Anyway, he's an old man now and all he cares about is where his next drink is coming from.'

Before we say goodbye, Joyce invites me to come and eat in her new restaurant, as soon as it opens. I'm delighted to accept.

When we come back to Nairobi again five months later the restaurant is supposed to open. Klaus and I ring up Joyce and now we are on the way to have lunch there. I can't wait to see how it looks.

We drive through Nairobi's industrial park near the airport. The restaurant is supposed to be in the slum district on the edge of it. But it takes us hours to get there, stuck in heavy traffic amid stinking lorries all heading the same way. It's almost impossible to make any progress. Just a few kilometres takes two hours. Joyce has already called me on the mobile twice to ask what's keeping us.

Eventually we leave the tower blocks behind and find our-selves on the edge of the slum district, which turns out to be one of the better ones, not quite as filthy as some. We drive down a narrow little alleyway, gaped at by everyone we pass. We're looking out for Babylon, the name of the restaurant, among all the advertising hoardings. Then we spot Joyce waving frantically at us. We climb out and she throws her arms around us, saying, 'I've been waiting for you here since early morning! My sons have been laughing at me, saying I've imag-ined you were coming and I'd be better off inside working.' We apologise for being so late. Her two sons say hello. One of them is an artist, the other an electrician who runs the busi-ness. We enter the restaurant and I can hardly believe what this woman has managed to achieve. It's not actually due to open until next week but I can already imagine how it's going to do. Everything is laid out beautifully, the benches covered with blue leatherette and red-and-white checked tablecloths on every table, while the walls are covered with jolly cartoon characters: Tom and Jerry, or Obélix with his fat belly carry-ing a big platter of roast meat. There's a portrait of Bob Marley hanging behind the bar, and Joyce proudly tells us her younger son, the artist, painted it. There's loud pop music playing from speakers, all of which was set up by the other son, the electri-cian. The kitchen beyond is huge and equipped with vast pots and pans.

I'd love to see it all up and running, but Joyce needs to get the rest of her loan before she can organise an opening party with a big menu on offer. I have not the slightest doubt that it'll be extremely successful.

Joyce takes us round the corner to a little snack bar that is also part of her empire. Her two daughters-in-law run it. The few tables are all taken and there's not much standing room. Our host tells some of her customers to shove over and make room for us. All the time we sit there chatting, she is keeping a watchful eye on everything.

She laughs when she sees how much I'm enjoying my food and says, 'You're the first white people to eat in one of my restaurants. But you have to come back when the main one is up and running, then you'll have much more to choose from.'

As we leave I squeeze her hand and tell her how people back in Europe will be inspired by her life story and her success. I see a big smile break out across her tired face as she says, 'Thank you and come again.'

I promise myself I'll do just that next time I'm back in Nairobi.

Bernard and John – the gang bosses

Back now to Jamii Bora, and the first day that I met Joyce and heard her story. We're now introduced to the two young men in the room, the pair who sat there all along playing with their phones and looking bored. I turn first to Bernard, who's sitting next to me, unable to imagine what sort of story he's going to tell me.

'My name is Bernard and I'm twenty-eight years old,' he says in his soft voice. 'Here's what I've got to tell you: Jamii Bora came into my life at a time when nobody in Kenya had any use for me, nobody even wanted to know me.

'It was during the last spate of terrible riots after the 2007–8 elections, riots that John and I here were at least partly responsible for in the area where we lived. You have to understand that when we have elections the politicians are always on the lookout for people to support them and help them win. Here in the Kibera slums there are hundreds of thousands of people whose votes can easily be won with not very much money. We're from the Luo tribe, so we campaigned for the opposition. We got a gang together and worked the ground really hard, and reckoned when it came to voting day we were sure to win. Everything pointed that way. We'd been promised that when we won the election, we'd get jobs. That was how we got our gang of 213 people together and got them to make people vote the right way. But watching the TV on election night we could see that the politicians were all going wild and realised that there was some sort of electoral fraud going on. Gradually we could see that the victory we had all counted on wasn't going to happen and we began to lose all hope.

'We sat there watching the votes come in until three in the morning, still imagining that somehow or other we could win. But when it finally became clear that the election had been stolen, we just went crazy with anger. We all got together and started marching into the centre of the city, smashing anything in our path. We set fire to car tyres and set up roadblocks.' He points at his friend and says, 'John here was the general and I was his adjutant. We smashed up water pipes and electricity lines as we fought our way into the city centre to the main polling station. The whole gang took on the police. Five of us were shot dead. When we finally realised we weren't going to get any closer to the city centre, we retreated to Kibera to think about what to do next. The police wouldn't dare follow us back here. Over the next few days, they stopped any young people trying to get into the centre of the city, and gradually food supplies in the slums started to run out. Even young men went hungry because there was simply nothing more to steal.

'One day, dying of hunger and racked with hatred, we decided to stage a raid on the main market where lots of Kikuyu came to sell meat, fish and vegetables. The market stalls were all made of wood and our plan was to smash them up and then set fire to them, then to take over the land they sat on and become landlords. We thought that would be a fitting punishment for the Kikuyu for stealing the election.

'We set out that night armed with stones and pangas, but when we got to the market we found it guarded by some tough Masai warriors who had good weapons and knew how to fight. We tried charging them but were beaten back. The same thing happened the next night. The third day we tried again, fought really hard, and managed to set fire to one side of the market, which gave us a way through to plunder what we could before the rest all burnt down. We were determined to take the land, divide it up among us and build ourselves huts. But we had no money and we still had the police to deal with.

'Then one day a guy called Andrew mentioned Jamii Bora. At first I wasn't even willing to listen, but he kept on about it every day and said, "Look, Bernard, I know you well. I was born in Kibera too and there's only one thing I have to say to you: What you're doing is wrong and it's dangerous: you're stealing from people and taking away their livelihoods. It can't go on. One of these days somebody's going to shoot you too. I can make you a better offer. Come with me to Jamii Bora, they'll give you something to eat and food to bring back to the slum and distribute. You know the people here, they're afraid of you and that's why you are the only ones who can come and go freely here. Neither the police nor the Red Cross can help the starving people here because they're all afraid. And it could be a big opportunity for you to do something good."

'I was doubtful, but then I reckoned that this Jamii Bora guy was Luo just like me and just wanted us to hand out food to women and children. John wasn't interested either at first and warned me against leaving the gang. He said it might be a trap. But I'll let him tell you his side of the story.'

I turn to John, interested in what he has to say. He's a bit smaller than Bernard and seems more reluctant to talk. There's something about him that puts me on edge. But when he starts talking I'm surprised at how quiet and gentle his voice is. I even have to ask him to speak up a bit because I can hardly make him out. Susanne, the woman from Jamii Bora, smiles and says, 'He's our quiet man.' But the name doesn't exactly fit with what he's telling me.

'My name's John. I'm thirty-two years old. Before we got to know Jamii Bora our life was anything but easy. From 1995 to 2008 I was the general of the hardest, most feared gang in Kibera. It was thirteen years of hell. During all that time

Carrying gourds, Himba style.

The local women are amazed at the first sight of our camels.

A Himba woman carrying her child in a goatskin pouch.

A roaring waterfall at Epupa.

A donkey ride to the well.

Himba children in a dried river bed.

Fetching drinking water is a job for the girls.

My 'home' for a few weeks.

The camp fire is also our kitchen.

Market women in Nairobi.

The ironing man with his wooden ironing board.

Washing done by slum women hangs on
balconies in a middle-class district.

Matatus struggles with the chaotic Nairobi traffic.

A view over Kibera slum and school.

On our way to meet the slum dwellers.

Irene in her garden.

Doreen and her son, outside their home.

A Mathare United FC training session.

Innocent and Joseph – Mathare United FC stars.

My former husband Lketinga, back in 1987.

Me with my daughter Napirai, in Barsaloi, 1989.

A warm reunion with Mama.

Mama is delighted to see her granddaughter Napirai again.

Napirai with her youngest half-sister and her proud father.

Most of the family gather outside James's house.

Napirai with her devoted cousin Diego.

Papa Saguna's daughter along with little Albert and Saguni.

Mama.

James in his house, with Papa Saguna on the
left and Lketinga's wife on the right.

Saguna and Shankayon, Napirai's half-sister.

A final meeting with Mama before we leave.

I never once went to visit my mother while, as her youngest son, it should have been my duty to look after her.

'I led a nocturnal life, never knowing what would happen next. The young men like me, living in the slums, were only interested in smashing things out of frustration with our lives. We were bad to know and most of the trouble was caused by us. I was a gang boss. I'm telling you, Corinne, it's no easy job running a gang of 213 hoodlums, gaining respect from men who were all on drugs. You've no idea what it's like trying to control the potential for violence.

'When this guy Andrew from Jamii Bora turned up in April 2008, he was taking one hell of a risk. I didn't want anything to do with him, but he kept on. He wasn't easily scared off. And I'm glad. Today when I look back, I think that was God at work. I was still sceptical, but gradually Jamii Bora became part of my life. After he persuaded Bernard and me to distribute food in the slums, we decided to go along with them, if only because it might get us jobs.

'A couple of weeks later the same people came to us and said they wanted to reopen the market again, which caused a right stink among the gang because it was ours, we had conquered it, and five of us had been killed in the process. We were landlords!'

John's voice has got louder and there is a cold glint in his eyes that makes it all too easy to imagine what he must have been like at his worst.

'We had a long talk,' he goes on. 'It was only when they said they would talk to previous owners of the market area and make sure that we would have a share in the new business that we came to any sort of compromise.'

I can't help asking the two of them how they managed to free themselves from drug addiction.

John looks me right in the eye and says, 'Listen, Corinne, I was tough, people were afraid of me. If you want to be a gang leader you've got to set the right example. I was the first to take drugs when none of the others had ever even seen any.

When they got into marijuana I was already shooting heroin. There are only two rules: if you want respect, you have to be the bravest and the toughest. We looked after all the money, but we also divided it out equally. Some don't do that, and it's a mistake. They pay for it in the end.

'When the chaos had calmed down we went to see Jamii Bora and talked over with Andrew how we might borrow money. He explained it all and how people had to vouch for one another and take responsibility for their debts. Obviously he was only talking to me and Bernard. There was no way he could talk to the rest of the gang. But that's the way of the world, isn't it? If you want to get something done, you have to talk to the bosses, even if they're government ministers or presidents or whatever,' he says with a wink. 'But I didn't really trust Andrew. I didn't even like going to his office. It could have been a trap and I would have lost face with the gang. If it had all gone wrong I would have been tossed aside like a nobody.

'But Andrew was as good as his word, and eventually we organised three groups of five gang members willing to vouch for each other, each one of them willing to take responsibility for the debts of the others. Even though I still had doubts about the whole business we all managed to put aside 5,000 shillings [€50] each, went back to Jamii Bora and could hardly believe it when they allowed each of us to borrow double that much. All of a sudden each group had 50,000 shillings [€500]. It was incredible.'

I can imagine how it must have been for these kids suddenly to have a proper sum of money in their hands for the first time in their lives.

'The first thing we did,' John continues, 'was to take our car down to the bar and say, "Hey guys, it's party time." Bernard turned up too, but then Andrew came as well and told us in no uncertain terms that the money was supposed to be spent on setting up a business, not squandered on drink and drugs. I turned to him and said: "Excuse me, but that's not how I see it. We saved up and now we've got double our money. Anything else is your problem." But then Andrew said that if we paid back the money, we could have double it again: 20,000 shillings [€ 200]. It made no sense to me, but all of a sudden the only figure anybody could think of was the 20,000 shillings. All of a sudden the 10,000 we had in our pockets wasn't enough. Think how drunk we could get on twice that amount! We immediately started trying to work out what we could do to get to the 20,000. It was enough to send you mad. Of course, none of us were interested in actually working, all we wanted was to get more money.

'So we sat down and talked it over and then decided we could make metal chests, the sort everybody needs to have in their hut to put food or clothing in so it'll keep dry in the rainy season and so they can lock them up. So we spent money on the raw materials and went to work. At least a group of thirty-six of us did. Most of the rest were too afraid of being shot by the police or just didn't want to give up drugs.

'The problem was though that wherever we went people were still scared of us. Nobody believed we wanted to work. You need to understand, Corinne, after what we'd done – things so bad I don't even want to talk about them – it was really hard for anyone to trust us. What we'd done were so terrible that nobody could easily forgive us, even though we didn't show our faces as openly as we do today. Not enough time had gone by. But we worked hard and made one chest after another, selling each one for 1,500 shillings.

'Since April 2008 we've managed to build up a proper business. I scarcely recognise myself when I look in the mirror. The rings around my eyes have gone, the wrinkles have vanished. Even the district officer, who knew us all and knew how wicked we'd been, could hardly believe the change that had come over us. We talk about it with him a lot. Lots of people don't believe that it's all because of Jamii Bora. Hey, y'know, we're like honest businessmen!

'By August we'd paid back the loan we got in April and

actually did get 20,000 shillings. By then we had no more doubts. Imagine, Bernard and I currently have a loan of 150,000 shillings [€1,500], because we have so many orders coming in. We're making guttering and water butts so people can collect rainwater. Business is good. I'm a happy man.

'I've even made up with my ex-girlfriend, with whom I had a son back in 2004. It took me three months to persuade her to come back to me, but now we've got a daughter too.

'In July 2008, four months after we started working with Jamii Bora, I went back to see my mother for the first time in thirteen years. She had found it really hard being cut off from her youngest son and then reading in the newspapers what a bad lad I'd become. People had told her the only time she'd ever see me again was when I was dead. She was delighted that I had come back to see her. I told her everything and she sat there and cried for three days. Then I told her about Jamii Bora and she said, "Introduce me to this man who has had such a good influence on you!"'

And we all burst out laughing.

I ask him if he is regularly in touch with her now and he says, 'Yeah, yeah, I ring her ever day. Never a day passes but I call her at least once. She's really proud of me. I can tell you, Jamii Bora didn't just change my life, it saved it.'

As we leave I ask John if he never worries that he'll fall back into the bad old ways. He smiles and tells me emphatically, 'No way. Not a chance. I'm a happy man these days. Once upon a time, I didn't even understand what that meant. I live near Kibera and when I get home my children greet their papa. For me that's as good as it gets.'

No sooner has John finished speaking than I notice a bit of a fuss going on behind me. Ingrid Munro, the Swedish-born woman who started all this, the one they all call 'Mama', has entered the room. She's unprepossessing in her appearance.

Her long grey, almost white, hair is tied back behind her neck, leaving her clear blue eyes as the centre of attention. We say hello and she immediately starts telling me, in a slightly hoarse voice, how it all began. She is very casual in her story-telling which is filled with anecdotes, many of them, despite the tragedy that lies behind them, funny enough to make us laugh. She is sixty-nine and really ought to be retired, were it not for the fact that the beggars whose lives she changed won't let her go. 'But Mama can never retire,' they keep saying. 'What would we do without our Ingrid?'

'But,' she adds, 'I deliberately built this organisation up so that lots of the younger people would be capable of doing what I did. It's not like it used to be in the old days, when we were a "beggar women's club". It started out as fifty street beggars. In the beginning I would take all the money myself, spread it out on the bed in the evening, count it up and write it all down,' she says, reminiscing with a smile on her face.

'Now these women represent the core of the biggest micro-finance organisation in Kenya and perhaps the best known in the whole world. But they're the ones who deserve the praise, not me. I just showed them the ground rules, got them moti-vated and then lent a guiding hand. We were never afraid of hard work or problems along the way, even though some people thought we were mad. We've given loans to thieves, beggars and prostitutes, because in the end they're all human, have children to feed and a right to free themselves from poverty. None of them have become what they've become because they wanted to. Nobody is born a thief or a prostitute. Look at these two young men, John and Bernard: they were right hooligans and now they're worthwhile fellow citizens. But there were problems enough in the early days and more than a few things went wrong. Lots of the women got drunk often and whenever there was something to discuss, they all started talking at once. Believe me, I know each one of them personally and we've been through a lot together,' Ingrid says with a laugh.

'It was all because of one seven-year-old street child that I got to know any of them. He approached my husband and me one day on the street. We could see he had been wounded and we took him in. Eventually we adopted him. But even so, he ended up back on the street in an attempt to find his little brother. That was how I first came into contact with the women who lived out on the streets. At first it was very hard to get to know them, to gain their confidence and trust. It would never have happened without the child. It took us four years to find his brother. It turned out he had been thrown into jail when he was just four years old – can you believe it? It took ages for us to get him out and then adopt him too. The poor child was delighted to get out of jail and have a mother again. Every child needs and wants a mother, no matter what colour, size or shape she might be. The main thing is to have someone you can call "mother", someone to love you.'

We thank her for telling us her story but we have to say our farewells because there is a Jamii Bora project to see a few hours' drive away.

In my eyes, for all the work she has done to help people out of poverty, for the intelligent and ingenious model she's devised to loan money to the most desperate people in society, giving them a chance to improve their lives, Ingrid Munro deserves a Nobel Prize.

KAPUTIEL TOWN – AN AFRICAN MIRACLE

We're off to visit Kaputiel Town, a unique township inhabited by former tramps, beggars, prostitutes or just poor people escaped from some slum or other. What makes them special is that they have all picked themselves up by their bootlaces and escaped poverty. Now they live in houses of their own, each with three bedrooms, running water, a bathroom and electricity. Hearing about it in advance makes it sound like a fairy tale and I'm eager to see it in real life.

The countryside gets more open and more beautiful the further we get from Nairobi. We're heading towards Masai country. Before long we come across the first nomadic herders with their cattle. My heart leaps: this is my Africa; I can feel it deep down. We pass hundred of grazing camels – I've never seen so many together before. The contrast with the hectic pace of life in Nairobi, which I've had to get used to over the past few weeks, is a huge relief. Far ahead in the distance we can see the flat, snow-covered summit of Kilimanjaro. Just the sight of it makes my heart beat faster and the palms of my hands go damp as my mind drifts back to 2003 when I climbed the great mountain. Looking at it now, so majestic in the distance, I can scarcely believe I once stood on the top of it. That was an adventure I shall remember all my life, even if it really was too much for me. As we ascended the peak I wondered for the first time in my life what on earth I was doing. That's not to say that I wasn't proud of myself afterwards. That experience, just like my trek through the semi-desert of northern Namibia, was just another challenge I had to rise to.

We climb out of the car to feel a strong warm wind blowing in our faces. Already there are several women waiting to meet us who all throw their arms around us in greeting. There is also a tall Masai man among them. It's difficult to understand what they're saying, though, because the wind blows their words away and I can't exactly stick my ear in the face of the mzee, which is what they call the most respected elders here. As far as I can work out the big Masai man seems to be the local leader. He is wearing a grey suit with a green hat and has an attractive, noble face. He stands there, his eyes watching me calmly and attentively, as he waves his stick in one direction then another, telling us, 'That's going to be the administration building, over there is the well, and that's the primary school beyond it.' He pauses for a few seconds and then adds, 'There are already a hundred and fifty families here, about six hundred people. When all the houses have been completed and all the infrastructure is up and running, there should be some two thousand families here.'

While he's talking a Masai woman comes up and greets me, wearing the traditional ornaments around her neck and bangles on her arms and with a brightly coloured shawl around her shoulders. All the other women just stand around listening. The atmosphere surrounding here is very pleasant. The people in this township come from different ethnic backgrounds but live together like one big family. It seems, however, that it's a pleasant break in their daily routine to have outsiders come and take an interest in their community. They are all obviously proud to live here.

To live here, they have to meet certain criteria in order to be considered for a house. They all have to have come from the slums and be able to pay back all their loans through their own income. They also have to save up some capital of their own. A three-bedroomed house with a shower, running water and a few hours of electricity a day costs 150,000 shillings [€1,500] unfurnished. It may seem cheap but for the people here it means they have to work hard and save. They also have to pay a small amount of interest on their loan over ten to fifteen years. When I think back to the stories I've heard of women who've taken a year and half to save the equivalent of just €35, I can hardly imagine how these former street women and beggars managed it. But then those still living in the slums have to pay their landlords rent to keep a roof over their heads, even if it is only a rusty piece of corrugated iron, and the shacks they live in will never belong to them. The worst thing is that the real price per square metre in the slums can be more expensive that in better-off districts.

Three Fishes – the foundation stones of Claris's house

First of all I'm taken to a shop belonging to a woman called Claris. She's been part of the project from the beginning, back when it was just the fifty beggar women. She's a sturdily built woman of about fifty with a round face, short curly hair and hard-looking eyes that reflect a life of hardship and deprivation. Her temporary shop is in a building that is intended one day to become the township supermarket. She uses the front room as the shop and the back room as her store. There's shelving behind the counter with tubes of Colgate toothpaste, toothbrushes, soaps, Vaseline, deodorants, washing powder and even Always sanitary pads 'for the modern woman'. Another set of shelves has tins of Kimbo lard, bottles of oil, packets of maize flour, rice, biscuits and matches, all stacked high. In front of the counter there is a jute sack full of little dry fish, with a tin can, which is obviously used to measure out each portion to sell. Next to the fish are sacks of kidney beans, tomatoes, onions and potatoes, while in the cooler rear of the shop are piles of cabbages.

All of this obviously reminds me of the four years I spent back in Barsaloi among the Samburu when I opened a shop of my own. Back then it was the only shop for miles in the wasteland and I sold the same sorts of things Claris has on display here. I had to weigh out several hundred tons of sugar and flour by hand every day because it wasn't packaged up back then the way it is now. I didn't stock toothbrushes or toothpaste because the Samburu used a special wooden stick to clean their teeth, which didn't stop them from having the whitest of teeth. And none of the women would have had a clue what to do with a sanitary towel. But maybe that has changed now too.

Claris tells me proudly, 'My sons and I make a good living out of this shop. I have Ingrid to thank for it all. I had been living on the street for fifteen years before she came to my rescue, inspiring me to save money so that eventually she could give me a small loan. She always had faith in me. I started out really smalltime, with just three fish, which I fried and cut up into small pieces to sell. And now look what I've built up from those humble beginnings.' She waves an arm expansively around her shop before adding, 'And that's not all. Oh no. I'm lucky enough to have a lovely house too. Come and see. I'll tell you how I met Mama Ingrid and what happened next.'

Her house is very nice indeed, clean, filled with uphol-stered furniture, a table and chairs and a wooden sideboard, all covered with little pink or white crocheted throws. We sit down in the living room, the mzee opposite me. Before Claris can start to tell her story, the women clap and sing in praise of Jamii Bora.

'Corinne, I was married but my husband turned me out because I only gave birth to boys. Five boys was too many, he said. Boys only cost money. You couldn't get a good price for them when they got married, unlike girls. He threw me and the children out of the house and we ended up on the streets of Nairobi, while he found himself a new, younger wife. I told myself, "Well that's it, Claris, you'll die out here on the streets." I met up with other women in the same situation as me. There were some fifty of us, all with children, all struggling just to stay alive, year after year.

'One day this white woman, Ingrid, came along and gave us

some money: sometimes it would be fifty shillings, sometimes a hundred. We looked forward to seeing her because to us she meant money, and money meant food. She always brought along her little adopted street child who was keen to make friends. It was through him that we got to really talk to her, because none of us spoke English, but we wanted her to keep giving us money. After a few weeks she brought along another woman who could translate into Swahili. Ingrid told us she couldn't go on just giving us money. If she gave us money on a Monday, by Wednesday it was all gone. One day she would go back home to Sweden and then there would be nobody to come and look after us. She told us we would have to change our lifestyle. We said, "How can we do that, when we have nothing? No money, no home, nothing but the streets where we sit and beg. Give us more money, give us shillings." But Ingrid was convinced there had to be a way to get us off the streets. She would come up with something.

'A few days later she came and told us a lorry was going to come to take us all to Soweto. "Soweto?" we said. "Where's Soweto and what are we going to do when we get there, with nowhere to live?"

'"You've no choice," she replied. "The government is no longer prepared to tolerate you out on the streets. There are some VIPs coming to Nairobi and they don't want them to see beggars on the streets. If you don't go, you'll be put in jail. They are putting up a big tent for you all to live in."

'None of us trusted her. We thought, maybe she's just going to tip us all into some river. Then the lorry came and they told us that if we didn't get in, we'd be taken off to jail. So we went to Soweto and all lived together with our children in this big tent. But you have to remember, we had all come from the streets: we had no sense of decency or respect. We spent all the time arguing and fighting among ourselves in front of the children.

'After two weeks Ingrid decided things couldn't go on the way they were. She found a separate nook or cranny for each of us. We got shacks or huts, a bed and a blanket. But she was adamant that we had to do some sort of work. "All of you must have some skill, something you can do to earn money," she told us.

'I said to her, "I come from near Lake Victoria and I know lots about fish."

'So she gave me some money and I started out with those three fried fish. Ingrid told me that every day I had to save a little and give that money to her to look after. If I did that long enough, she would lend me twice what I had saved. I wasn't at all sure I believed her but I tried hard to save, even though it was very difficult with the tiny sums I was earning. But by the end of a year I had saved a thousand shillings and indeed she lent me double that. I could hardly believe my good fortune. I bought more little fish, fried them and sold them. At last my children could afford enough ugali to eat. A year on, I had 2,500 shillings saved, and Ingrid lent me 5,000. Before long I was able to borrow 10,000.

'I can tell you, Corinne, it felt like a dream come true to have so much money in my hands. Obviously I had to spend more paying off the bigger loans, but the more I had to sell, the more money came flooding in. I got the idea of setting up a shop and with the next loan I rented and set up a market stall. Business was good and more and more of my customers wanted to know how I'd done it. I found myself giving inter-views, telling people my life story. Eventually the man who owned the stall had enough and threw me out. He was jealous and thought I was being paid to talk to people. Back out on the streets I started up again frying fish and selling them, but that was no longer enough for me, so I prayed, "Dear Lord, please help me so I can get a house of my own and open a shop. Please, Lord, have mercy on Claris."

'And indeed I managed to get to the next level for a loan and got 150,000 shillings [€1,500]. With that I was able to get hold of four tiny pieces of land with stone houses on them. By the time I got to the next level I had enough to two equip two of the little houses as a restaurant offering fish, ugali, vegetable and soft drinks. One of my sons still runs that restaurant as manager. One of my other sons has got a mobile phone shop and another one is learning to be a tailor. Son number five has a stall on the market place finding jobs for housemaids. Not one of my children ever went to school but even so today they are successful businessmen. Over the years I've put ever more money aside until eventually I could afford a house like this,' she says, beaming with pride.

'The boy who wants to be a tailor works with me here in the shop. But when he has time, he gives other lessons in cloth cutting. We want to share our good fortune. And let me tell you, Corinne, nowadays when I go back to where I came from they all treat me with great respect and say things like, "Whatever happened to Claris? How did she get to be so rich?" They don't understand. To tell the truth, I don't really understand it myself. Sometimes I have to ask myself, "Are you really the same Claris who used to beg on the streets?"'

She breaks out into laughter and we all join in.

Hers really is an amazing rags-to-riches story, one to warm your heart, especially when you hear her tell it. There's something infectious about the woman's courage.

'When I go back and see people in the countryside,' she says, 'I invite them to come for tea and tell them my story. They all treat me as if I was a government minister.'

We all burst out laughing again.

'Some of them even come down here to see this big house I have, because they can't quite believe it. They gape at my fine furniture, and I sit there and tell them, "Yes, this is mine, my house, all earned and bought without a husband. Claris's house!" The mzee nods and smiles and all the women standing around us burst into applause.

'I tried to motivate as many people as possible back home on the shores of Lake Victoria, to get them to join up with Jamii Bora. But for most of them the office was just too far away. But then I had a chat with Ingrid and today there's a branch up there too, all because of me. I'm really happy about that and sometimes I go up there to tell other people my story and encourage them. It's just amazing what I've been able to do with my life thanks to this organisation. Even my sons sometimes can't believe it and pray to God that it will all continue.

'There's one last thing I want to say: I am determined to help others and be charitable. When I see hungry children or old people back home in the Rift Valley I always give them some maize flour, because I can never forget the times when I was dependent on others. That is my way of giving thanks to God for getting Claris off the streets. And another thing: if my husband back then hadn't thrown me out I would never have achieved all this. I'm rich and my boys have all done well. I have had good fortune. May God bless Mama Ingrid and Jamii Bora so they can carry on helping people.'

Once again everybody is singing and clapping as we make our way to the house of the next woman I am due to interview.

How Jane got out of prostitution
Jane wears a flame-red sport shirt over her skirt and her thick hair stands out in a halo round her head. She is young with a genuine, open smile. But she has a scar running from her forehead down to the side of her nose. It is most noticeable when she is speaking. But when her eyes light up and she breaks into laughter, you hardly notice it at all. Jane's house is superficially similar to Claris's but the decoration is more striking. Pink is the dominant colour. The furniture is all covered with pink throws while the walls are decorated with white embroidery hangings. There's a modern electric sewing machine in one corner.

We sit down on the upholstered furniture round the table to listen to Jane's story. I continue to be amazed at how frank women here are in telling their life stores. They aren't put off even by the presence of the elderly Masai gentleman. It seems nobody here is embarrassed by anything.

'I had a traditional wedding in Nakuru when I was just

eighteen,' Jane starts by saying. 'I had my first baby when I was nineteen – a little girl. A year later I was pregnant again. My mother took ill when I was heavily pregnant and I had to go and help her with the housework. So I had my second baby in her house. A week later my mother was dead. First of all I had to organise her funeral before I could return home to my husband with the two children. But when I got home I got a terrible shock. While I'd been gone, my husband had married another woman and brought her home to our house to live with us. At first I tried to get along with my "co-wife" but she was very rude to me and my children. After six weeks I took my two little girls and moved out, travelled to Nairobi and found somewhere to live in the Mathare slum.

'But with two little girls to look after I couldn't get a job. Nobody would hire me and so as a last resort the only thing I had to sell was my body. Lots of young mothers end up doing the same thing. I got together with some other women – there was just over two hundred of us – and together we did it properly: we started a properly organised sex business. I lived with five other women in one house and we all helped each other out. It wasn't an easy life but we made money. From 1995 to 1998 that was how I lived, doing this job, even when I got pregnant again. If you don't work, you don't eat.

'Then in 1998 Jamii Bora opened a branch here in the Mathare slum and one day one of their organisers came along to tell us about their work. She said that if we really wanted to and tried hard enough we could change our way of life. But we didn't believe her and refused to listen to her. But she wouldn't give up. She said we were good mothers and were only doing the job we did to feed our children. She didn't criticise us, she just said she wanted to help. But she also told us over and over how dangerous the job we were doing was. Some of the women had undergone the traditional genital mutilation, which made the sex worse for them. After months of her coming back again and again to visit us we eventually gave in and said, "Okay, you show us what you can do to help us." That was when she told us about Mama Ingrid, the white lady, and said she would ask her for advice.'

All the time she is talking I'm staring in amazement at the sparkle in her eyes. She's telling us all this frankly and honestly without complaint or feeling sorry for herself. The other women are all intent on listening to her too, just as they were with Claris.

'Before the Jamii Bora woman left us that day,' Jane continues, 'she asked if we had any other skills or any handiwork we were good at. Out of the two hundred young mothers only seven put their hands up to say they could do something like cutting hair, sewing clothes or making beads. But the woman told the others not to worry and said, "There's no need to be jealous. Set out everything you own on the table and we'll share it all out. Then in the next day or so I'll come back with an answer."

'And Mama Ingrid decided to give us a loan so we could rent a room, set up a couple of sewing machines and everything we need for a dressmaking business, for a beauty parlour and a hairdressing salon. The ones who knew how to do something taught the others. And while we were learning an adviser came to teach us how to save money too. It's hard work as a grown-up to learn how to put away a little every day from the tiny amount of money you earn. Up until then we'd lived and worked one day at a time but now we were learning how to save for a better tomorrow. Only ninety-five out of the two hundred single mothers joined in. The others weren't interested in the hard life that came with working and saving.

'I started in 1999. To start with I went into a shop and asked the price of the cheapest sewing machine. It was 4,000 shillings. That meant I would have to save 2,000. I used the money to buy a treadle sewing machine and three second-hand dresses. Back home I cut them up and made them into six skirts for little girls, which I could sell for 150 shillings each. That meant I now had my own sewing machine and 900 shillings in my pocket. I was very proud, even though I was still living in a shack in the Mathare slum with my children and had not a stick of furniture. With the next lot of money I earned I bought a bed and a mattress and some cooking pots so I could make dinner at home. Things were a little better than they had been but still not exactly good, as when the rains came water still flooded into the shack. That only made me work harder. I sewed and sewed and with the next loan I got I started making jewellery too, and that sold well. So I just kept on at it and built it up slowly, getting bigger and bigger loans. By now I was up to level 13 and could borrow 600,000 shillings. As a result I've been living in this nice house since 2002 and my eldest children – there are four of them now – go to school. And to think it all started eleven years ago with a loan of just 4,000 shillings,' she said with a beaming smile.

I'm hugely impressed that in just eleven years, despite all her hardships, this woman has managed to turn €40 into €6,000.

'You know what I think,' says Jane, 'I think God sent Mama Ingrid to Kenya to tell us that we don't have to be poor and ignorant. It was just that nobody had taught us what to do. Now we know and we can get on with it. You can see how my life had changed completely. Here I am today, the proud mother of two boys and two girls. They love me and I love them, and I am hopeful that there is a great future for all of us. I was even brave enough to go and take an HIV test. The result was positive but I just have to live with that as best I can. I've achieved great things here. None of us go hungry and there's no other stress in our lives any more. Stress can make HIV turn into AIDS. Everybody knows how I used to live and about my illness but they just accept me the way I am,' she tells us almost merrily. She has such an infectious laugh that we all find ourselves joining in, even if there's not exactly anything to laugh at.

'Once upon a time,' she goes on, 'I wanted to be a doctor but it simply wasn't possible. But today I'm almost better than a doctor because I give advice to other HIV-positive people, warn young girls about the dangers of infection, and give them sewing lessons. Before I had got the money together to buy this house I prayed to God and promised Him that if I managed to get myself out of the slums I would take two young girls with me and teach them. When I finally got the house and could afford a new electric sewing machine I kept my promise. Those two girls learnt all I could teach them and now I'm training another Masai girl. My oldest daughter is nearly eighteen and I'm proud to say she's completed secondary school. Maybe she'll end up a doctor or something like that. My dreams live on.'

I ask her if she has any dreams for herself and she laughs and days, 'Of course. Lots. First of all I'd like a nice car to park outside the door.' When we all stop laughing, she adds in a serious voice, 'The very least I want to do is pay off the loan on the house. But my biggest wish is to have grandchildren, though I've told my daughters not to get pregnant too soon – they should finish their studies first. But I just hope I'm still around by then and don't depart this world as young as my own mother did. I wish God had let her live longer so that she could have seen how well things turned out for her daughter. She would have been proud of me.'

We all applaud and I can't help but be moved by her unaffected optimism. She gets up and lays out some glass beads on the table, smiles and says, 'Right, the shop is open for business.'

Klaus and I pick out some nice pieces of jewellery. I mention that I must choose a necklace for my daughter and all of a sudden everybody wants to know how old she is and how many children I have. They're all amused when I say I have just the one. 'Oh, only one!' they exclaim. I get some photos out of my handbag and they all fuss over them, saying, 'Oh, isn't she pretty! But why is she so brown? She looks half-African.' That's when I take out the other photo, show them my former husband and his family, the manyatta I built, and tell them my own story. That amuses all of them and they start talking all at once. The mzee gives me a long look and smiles as he flicks through the photos.

Jane exclaims, 'You absolutely have to bring your daughter to see us. I invite you to come to my house for a holiday. I've even got running water and a toilet. You absolutely have to come. You're Kenyans!'

She fetches a guestbook for us to sign. Then the Masai man gets to his feet and asks us to follow him. We walk out into the blazing sunshine. He leads us into a sort of garden behind the building facade and invites us to plant a tree. They've got everything all prepared and all Klaus and I really have to do is think up something nice to write on a wooden board that they will place next to the tree.

As we go through the motions of planting the tree all the women start their singing and hand-clapping again. It's a very jolly atmosphere and I feel quite honoured to be allowed to plant a tree with my name on it here in this little settlement among such a special community.

As we set out from Kaputiel Town back towards Nairobi the children are just getting out of school and the streets really come alive. There are at least a dozen children in coloured uniforms pouring into their new homes.

All the way back to Nairobi I can't help thinking about Ingrid Munro, this remarkable woman whose involvement in these people's lives has done them all so much good. And I have to congratulate those she helped too. who have put such discipline, energy and sheer love of life into dragging themselves out of poverty.

Five months later we're back in Kaputiel Town again. Nobody knows we're coming; we want it to be a surprise. I'm hoping to see at least Claris and Jane again. Our car comes to a halt outside Claris's shop, throwing a huge cloud of dust into the air in this arid landscape. Everything seems rather dead, but then gradually a few curious heads poke out and all sorts of people, none of whom I recognise, appear. Inside Claris's shop I find one of her sons, who immediately dashes to the telephone to call his mother and within minutes she comes running from her house to meet us with a huge grin on her chubby face.

'No, Corinne, it's really you, come back to see us again. God bless you!' She throws her arms around me like I'm her long-lost daughter. She's genuinely thrilled, which is very moving, but then these people are so thankful for the good luck they've made for themselves that they want to share it with everyone.

'Klaus, Corinne, my friends, come, let's go into the house and have some tea.' Claris sends a boy to find Jane, who charges through the door just a few minutes later. She's got a smart new hairdo, and her eyes beam as soon as she sees me and Klaus. We're all hugging and kissing one another, but straight away she asks me, 'But where's your Samburu daughter? Why haven't you brought her?'

I tell her that we have just been to see her father but that she had to go back to Switzerland. That in itself interests them and they have loads of questions for me. While Claris fusses about, getting all her best china out, one of her neighbours she's told about us drops in. I show them all the pictures of our visit back to Barsaloi, which are all still on my camera, and we all sit and chat and laugh over tea and biscuits. It's just like one big family. Even Jane's children turn up. It's the school holidays. All they want to know is how far I've got with telling their story. They can't wait to see pictures of themselves in a real book.

Our surprise visit has worked out well. Everybody's happy. There's no sign of the difficult past that all these women had before they came here, no indication of all they went through over the years. They tell me that the township has grown. Another three families have moved in, all of them single mothers, who used to be either beggars or prostitutes and have hordes of children. It all seems miraculous, a sort of African fairy tale, but it's all based on self-discipline, hard work, an indomitable will to survive and a deep faith in God.

As we all hug each other again when we take our leave, I'm certain of one thing: I will never forget these women. They have shown me that nothing is impossible.

MATHARE UNITED — THE SLUMDOG FOOTBALL STARS

The international media has already carried stories about Mathare United, Kenya's most incredible football team, particularly in 2008 when they not only won promotion to the top flight but won the national league. The incredible thing about them is that all these professional footballers come from Mathare slum. They have quite literally pulled themselves up by their bootlaces. The secret to their success is nothing more than long years of self-discipline and hard training, and today they're reaping the rewards. As full-time professionals they get paid between €100 and €300 a month, depending on how long they've been with the team. To be entitled to those wages they not only have to train but must be actively involved in local society, because football players are supposed to set a good example for the youth in the slums. That means that every day after training they have to take on some other work, whether it's looking after old or sick people, telling people how to prevent AIDS or going to visit boys in jail. Sometimes they even clean the slum's streets.

There's no comparison with European footballers, who have contracts worth millions. Whatever they do after training, they certainly don't clean the streets.

Mathare United FC was founded in 1994 by Bob Munro, a former Canadian United Nations employee and the husband of Ingrid Munro. The players all came together through the

Mathare Youth Sports Association, which he also founded back in 1987. I was particularly interested to meet them because they have twice been nominated for the Nobel Peace Prize. I'm fascinated to learn about this unusual team, how they come to be in it, and how it all works.

We've got a meeting with Francis Kimanzi, the team coach, at 10 a.m. at their training ground.

Once again we have a driver come and pick us up from the hotel because the training ground is in a slum area we'd rather not have to travel to on our own. We slowly take the road out of our 'respectable' residential area and, as we've done so many times before, take the next turning at the crossroads to head towards the city centre. No matter what time of day we come by this crossroads we always find the same beggar kneeling on the ground on the stumps of his legs, giving a beaming smile to every driver that stops at the lights. He wears red plastic flip-flops on his hands so that they don't get too dirty when he has to scrabble a few metres to get to the coins thrown at him. The charisma this remarkably well-kempt man exudes is extraordinary. I've been watching him for weeks now and every time he sees us he greets us with a cheerful 'God bless you', whether we give him money or not.

I ask the driver if he knows anything about him. 'Yes,' he says, 'He's a lawyer by training, who lost both his lower legs in a motorbike accident. He's been begging here for years now. The police let him be. He has to earn his money like this because he can't work any more and doesn't have anyone to look after him. And he has a wife and three children to support.'

Two days later I see him without the slightest show of embarrassment laughing and playing with his eight-year-old, who drops by his 'workplace' on the way home for school. I'm deeply moved by the sight, which seems to show once again just how strong people can be when fate deals them a bad hand. This man seems happy, despite the loss of his legs and the fug of exhaust smoke that envelops him from dawn to dusk.

Shortly after we pass him we end up stuck in a traffic jam, barely crawling along. Overcrowded matatus, which is what they call the communal taxis here, squeeze past our car with only centimetres to spare. I glance at my watch nervously as there seems no chance we're going to arrive at the training ground in time for our meeting. Eventually we reach a three-lane stretch of road with traffic police. We keep left and gradually begin to make progress. I take the opportunity to shoot a few photos as we drive along. Steven, our driver, moves out into the middle lane so I can get closer shots. We've barely gone two hundred metres when a hefty policewoman steps out in front of us. Steven slams on the brakes, rolls down the window and starts talking to her. At first we don't catch a word of it. Steven shrugs his shoulders as if the world's gone mad and gives an embarrassed laugh. We try to find out what's going on and the policewoman says, 'I'm going to have to arrest your driver for crossing the safety markings.' I have no idea what she's talking about, seeing as there are no markings at all anywhere on the road. To be sure, there are three lanes of traffic, but there is nothing to mark them apart. And that's not to mention the matatu drivers who don't have the slightest regard for any sort of lane discipline. But the policewoman isn't having any of it and insists: 'He has driven over the line and now he will get arrested.' She insists that he has crossed some imaginary line and will have to go to jail. We can drive on alone.

This is impossible: we have no idea where the training ground is and we hired the driver to get us there. We try to explain to the policewoman that this is crazy and we have an urgent need to get to an appointment. But it's no use. As we refuse to drive ourselves, she squeezes into the front passenger seat and insists Steven drive us all to the nearest police station. I'm still convinced we can sort it all out because the accusation levelled against him is completely absurd. How on earth in this chaos can somebody get arrested for simply changing lanes? It's a joke. Our driver reassures me that it won't take long and we should wait for him in the car. Time goes by and it looks like there's no way we're going to make our meeting with the coach. Klaus climbs out of the car to smoke a cigarette to calm his nerves, even though we're outside a police station and smoking in public has for some time now incurred a hefty fine. So while it may calm Klaus's nerves, it's doing the exact opposite to mine.

I give up and go into the station to see what's going on with our driver. Inside I hold out my hand to a heavy-set unfriendly woman who tells me she's the chief. She makes a point of ignoring my outstretched hand and carries on joking with her colleague who's responsible for all this. Then the two of them turn and grin at me and the chief says, 'Welcome to Kenya.'

I'm absolutely furious, even though I know that's obviously not going to help. Clearly they are looking for a bribe. It's coming up to the weekend and these two ladies are simply looking for a bit of extra spending money. It's not every day they have white tourists driving around this part of town. Because I was stupid enough to mention we had an important meeting they know that they can put the squeeze on us. Steven has to sign his name in a book, then they'll take his driving licence off him until his trial, he explains in embarrassment. It's a nasty little bit of business that could cost this man his job. We ring up his employers and explain the situation. They don't seem to think there's anything unusual about it at all. They tell us that if we hand over 5,000 shillings, Steven will get his licence back and we'll be able to continue. That's a small fortune for a driver in Kenya. Merely the fact that he had white people in his car could cost him a month's wages. Klaus and I put the money together and all of a sudden, it's as if nothing had ever happened.

We arrive late at the Mathare United clubhouse and training ground. I haven't been able to get over the incident on the way. But I know that in Africa it's important not to show stress when meeting people for the first time. Africans are very sensitive to others' attitudes and pick up straight away if somebody they meet is giving out bad vibes.

From the clubhouse they send us out on to the field where the trainer coaches the team every day between 10 a.m. and 1 p.m. The training ground is little more than a meadow. It rains so much here at the moment that the grass is very long, although there are also a few bare patches. Four men are sitting in the sun on a wooden bench next to a simple goal with loose netting that's obviously been darned in places, while out on the field twenty or so lads in yellow jerseys are going through training exercises. It all seems rather modest, with nothing to indicate that these players are in the top flight of Kenyan football. We ask for Francis, the trainer, and a rather quiet-looking man makes himself known and accepts our apologies for being late. I'm beginning to think it's not my day as he just sits there with the others watching the team training while we stand there in the baking heat. The young men out on the pitch take turns receiving the ball and shooting at the net. Out of the blue Francis points to the man sitting next to him and says, 'This man's the best goalkeeper in Kenya.' The man next to him replies, 'And this is the best and most sought after football coach in Kenya.'

I'm relieved that finally somebody has broken the ice and smile back and say, 'Well, that's why we're here. We want to talk to the best. We'd like to talk to some of the players too.'

But nobody replies. It's all gone silent again. Five minutes pass before Francis finally says, 'Why did you come now? Didn't anybody tell you that we train at this time of day? It's not a good time for interviews.'

Klaus tells him that a certain Mr Jecton who organised the meeting for us suggested this time. At this point the third man introduces himself as Mr Jecton. There follows a discussion between them in Kiswahili where all I can make out occasionally is my own name and the words 'White Masai'. The trainer turns to me then and asks me about my book and what other books I might be planning to write. He listens carefully for a bit and then says, 'Okay, I'll see what I can do for you. I'll have a word with the players. But if you're really interested in us and our football, you should come to a game. We're playing in the City Stadium the day after tomorrow.' He turns to Jecton and says, 'Give her your mobile number and sort it out with them.' Then he nods goodbye to us and walks off to talk to his players.

Unlike his coach, Jecton turns out to be extremely chatty. He tells me he's the financial head of Mathare United, though he used to be a player himself. We chat for a bit and agree to meet again the day after next, at the stadium.

The beautiful game

We're standing in a long queue waiting for our tickets. Klaus and I are the only white people. People stare at us a bit and ask which team we are here to support. We tell them 'Mathare United'. It seems we're the club's only fans in this queue. When we eventually get to the ticket desk we're told that VIP tickets have to be collected from another office on the other side of the stadium. So we have to queue up again, although this time the line is shorter. Most of those in this queue are wearing smart suits. The entry price is only €3 here while the ordinary seats cost just a third of that.

I have to admit that it's the first time in my life that I've actually been in a football stadium. The City Stadium only has 15,000 places but it still seems impressive to me. By the time the game starts only about one sixth of the seats are taken, although the stand where we are is relatively full. It's only later that I find out most Mathare United fans, who live in the slums, can't afford the price of a ticket or the bus journey to get here.

We're supposed to rendezvous with Mr Jecton but there's no sign of him. No sooner has the game begun than some twenty trumpet-like instruments erupt into a deafening din. Later, I learn that these things are called vuvuzelas, and they become more widely known after the 2010 World Cup in South Africa.

I'm almost driven out of my mind by just two of them in our immediate vicinity. I imagine that if I'd been at a World Cup game, my ears would have fallen off and my brain exploded.

Mathare United start well and are clearly the better team in the first half. But almost the entire audience are fans of their opponents, Gor Mahia FC, the other best-known club in Kenya. The former prime minister is their biggest fan. When Mathare get their first sight of the goal, I'm urging them on loudly, surprised at myself for getting so caught up in the game. The people sitting next to me smile and giggle a bit but obviously find me somewhat annoying. I get the feeling we might not be in the right seats. Down on the edge of the pitch there's a cameraman dashing back and forwards so quickly he's pulling the guy holding his cables along with him, which is quite amusing. I'm still sitting there cheering on my team when the cameraman rushes up into the stand and turns the camera on a couple in front of us before sticking it right into my face. A few days later down in the Mathare slum lots of people tell me they saw me on television.

Just before half-time the other side scores, but it's disallowed for being offside. Within seconds there's a near-riot going on by the side of the pitch and the police are moving in. It seems the local fans don't think it was offside and demand that the goal be allowed to stand. The man sitting next to me apologises for their behaviour and says these are the hardcore fans who can get violent at time. But the police take control of the situation and at half-time it's still 0–0.

Anyone who imagines the half-time break might be a time for the fans to relax has no concept of Africa. There are already about eighty people on their feet singing and dancing, doing a sort of Polonaise between the seats, blowing their vuvuzelas and singing their hearts out. I get an adrenalin rush from it all but just hope it stays peaceful. At one point they all get down on their knees with their arms around each others' shoulders, then all leap up into the air, turn right, put their hands to their heads as if saluting an officer and take a step forwards. To me it looks a bit silly and doesn't seem to have anything to do with football. We're watching it all with broad smiles on our faces when I spot Jecton on the left-hand side of the stand, waving at us. He comes over and says hello, telling us with a laugh that, as we guessed, we've been sitting in the wrong place, among the opposition fans, which wasn't very clever and could have been dangerous. He takes us up to a little box and introduces us to Bob Munro, who founded what was at the time the biggest sports club in Africa, MYSA, which eventually gave birth to the professional Mathare United Football Club. They obviously took the name from their idols, Manchester United.

Bob, a tall, thin man, with bright eyes behind rimless spectacles, introduces himself cordially, showing interest in me and my project. Before long we're all engaged in an animated conversation that lasts until the referee blows his whistle to start the second half. Bob tells me that the club will be celebrating its twenty-fourth anniversary in a few days' time. He invites us to the party. Bob promises he'll find me interesting people to talk to. There are going to be not just videos of old games but music and exhibitions of photography as MYSA also sponsors creative skills. I'm delighted to accept his invitation and can't wait to hear the team's stories.

The second half starts but there are only a few opportunities on goal and that's it. It seems to me that Mathare United play fairly while the other team commit lots of fouls. But on the other hand it also seems as if the referee is giving my team the benefit of the doubt. It ends in a no-score draw and when the whistle blows there's a rush for the exits. We take a safe rear exit having made an agreement to meet up with Bob at the party next Saturday.

A few days later I find out that we did well to avoid the exit crowds as there was a lot of trouble at the gates and as a result the next game was ordered to be played behind closed doors. That sounds to me like a shame, but I'm just pleased to have been at my first ever game and I'm already looking forward to the MYSA party and meeting the players.

The jubilee party

The party for the twenty-fourth anniversary of the MYSA
sports club is held on 6 March 2010 near the Huruma Stadium,
where there is a big, open but otherwise unremarkable square.
There is a trace of cloud in the sky but even so the sun is hot
above the hard, dusty square. It's about as big as two football
pitches and is ringed with tall grey apartment blocks with
washing hanging from the balconies. Some of them are only
half-finished and lots of people have climbed up to watch the
festivities down below. Everywhere I look there are children
and young people in the yellow MYSA shirts. They are all
members of the football club. I head for a shady open tent
where there are already several activities going on. There are
people explaining the risks of HIV and there is a doctor doing
tests on the spot for anyone who wishes. Apart from him
everything seems to be in the hands of fifteen- to twenty-year-
old teenagers.

The tent next door houses the photo exhibition. Frederick,
our guide, explains that the photos were also an MYSA project
which he himself has worked on since 2005. It all started with
twenty kids aged between twelve and seventeen from the
Mathare slum who were given simple cameras and told to take
snapshots of their everyday life. That produced a photo album
that sold around the world. The kids took snaps of their daily
life – or rather, their fight for survival – taken from their own
point of view. One example was of ten- and eleven-year-old
children looking after their younger siblings, or a seven-year-
old girl washing mountains of clothes with nothing more than
soap and her own bare hands, or other children cooking their
maize broth on charcoal stoves. Yet another photo shows kids
sleeping on top of rubbish tips.

There are pictures taken by children for children. Across
the tent are photos of the football team at sporting events or
doing cleaning duties in the slum, photos of fourteen-year-old
kids hanging around in tin shacks flooded by sewage or mud.
It's very moving to see everyday life from a child's point of

view. Frederick, the head of the photo project, is himself not yet twenty. He has some eighty kids involved. He tells me: 'I'd like to pass on to others what I've learned. We set up exhibitions of pictures of everything that goes on in the slums, so people can take stock of their lives and talk about them. Obviously we hope to sell a few of them as well,' he finishes with a friendly grin.

I'm still staring at the last few of these remarkable images when Bob Munro comes up and introduces himself cheerfully. He's the sort of man whom you immediately feel you've known for years. He takes me over to a tented area in which rows of chairs are marked 'reserved'. I've got a prime position, it turns out, right in the first row in front of the cups that are going to be handed out. A lot of the chairs are still unused at the moment, but before long they're filled up by local dignitaries and team sponsors.

With a broad smile on his face Bob says how great it is to see what all these kids have achieved. I congratulate him for what he has done, but he says, 'No, Corinne, it's not me, it's the kids. We started this all up twenty-four years ago when I was working in the Mathare slum as a representative of the UN. I saw little kids playing with a ball they'd made themselves in between heaps of rubbish and shards of broken glass. It moved me so much that I went over and promised the kids that if they cleared a proper space for them to play I would bring them a proper football. And to this day that's still the motto of the MYSA: "Do something for yourself first and then we'll help you with the infrastructure we've built up." Even the little ones soon learn that it's in their interest to do something for the common good. They don't earn money directly, but they become part of a club and can grow up to become a coach, a referee or even run one of the departments. Kids learn quick that it's worthwhile taking responsibility. In a country where the average age of the population is eighteen you soon learn how to do business and not just expect something from life. We have to teach them how to lead, how to act responsibly.

Most of our department heads or team coaches are just four-teen to sixteen years old. But they get engaged and get respect for it. Last year FIFA officially recognised our youngest foot-ball official. Her name is Charity Muthoni, she's just twelve years old and in her free time works with a hundred and thirty teams and a total of two thousand people. Isn't that incredible?'

It certainly is incredible to see how quickly these children mature compared with ours back in Europe, who at this stage still get driven to school or their local sports club and are taught by people years older than them. It's remarkable how self-assured these young people here are. Looking at them I can't help feeling that our affluence doesn't make our children freer, but instead makes them less self-assured, more depend-ent and smug.

Bob is still talking. 'MYSA isn't just a football or giant sports club. MYSA is designed to set a good example to the youngest kids. They need a goal in their lives to get them off the streets. In the slums you don't just need to educate the leaders of tomorrow, that's crazy, you need them today. Right now! The most important message MYSA sends out is: you can be what-ever you want to be, achieve whatever you want to – nothing's impossible – but everything takes really hard work. That's the only thing that makes life here different from anywhere else.'

There's a loudspeaker announcement that I can't quite make out, and Bob invites me to join him in welcoming the two teams of handicapped football players who are about to play a match. 'That's another thing, Corinne, we've seen to it that even those with disabilities get a chance in life. Sport makes them visible. People notice them. Previously the disabled were pushed aside or blocked in anything they wanted to do because their families were either ashamed of them or feared they'd get a bad reputation, which would damage the chances of their brothers and sisters finding a marriage partner. Here we give them a platform to be themselves. You're about to see a game played with real passion,' he tells me with a laugh.

Bob and I shake hands with the players, all of whom have

some physical or mental disability. You can feel how excited everybody is about the game. On the back of their shirts is the slogan: 'Give the young disabled a real chance.'

I stand next to the goal with a few other spectators. The keeper keeps jerking backwards and forwards and doesn't seem to be really following the game. He's wearing ordinary shoes with a silver stripe down them. It seems he has some mental handicap. A striker wearing two different football boots comes charging towards the goal, but the keeper manages to deflect his shot. The spectators applaud and he turns round to thank us just as another attacker takes the ball and lances it towards the net in a shot only just knocked away by one of the defenders. This particular defender caught my attention early on. He can only play with one foot because his other leg is deformed and just sort of hangs loosely so that he has to use a stick. It's quite incredible under the circumstances how deftly he manages to get around the pitch. He runs forwards then all the way back again, kicks the ball hard, heads it and even jumps, which takes my breath away. I can't get over his enthusiasm. He is easily the fastest player on the pitch. Even taking a free kick, he takes a run-up, leaning with both muscular arms on his stick before kicking the ball with his good leg.

There's a big African mama standing next to me who smiles and asks, 'Do you like the game?'

'It's great,' I tell her.

Then she says, 'The lad with the stick is my son. I'm so proud of him.'

I find myself thinking of Bob's words: just a few years ago, these kids would have been considered worthless. Now here's the mother of one of them standing proudly on the touchline watching him play! It's simply amazing.

Once again the ball is heading for the net and this time there's nothing the keeper can do. But instead of getting angry, he claps his hands in happiness for the opposite team. I can't get over the game, and when it's over and the player with the stick comes over to us, drenched in sweat, I tell him how much I enjoyed it, which makes him very happy.

Bob introduces me to his old friend and assistant Helge Søvdsnes. He is a formerly well-known Norwegian football player and has done wonders here. Now every year several MYSA teams of different ages go to Norway for the Norway Cup. For most of the kids it's the first time they've been out of the country, the first time they've been on a plane and the first time they've had the chance of spending a few days away from the slums. On many occasions the MYSA teams have even come out on top. They have a long list of victories, Helge says, and that includes the girls' teams.

'You know, Corinne, it was only in 1992 that women's football started in Kenya. Up until then you wouldn't have found a single girl who'd played. Back home in Norway we were world leaders in women's football. Our women won gold in the Olympics and the world title. I picked four of the best players out of those teams and brought them to Kenya. They spent a week in the slum girls' school doing training. One year, you wouldn't believe it, we had five thousand girls all playing in different leagues. Nobody here is talking about becoming world champions, it's all about winning the respect of the boys. And that we did. Look, over there two women's teams are playing and you can see how the boys and men are watching them almost in awe, clapping and cheering them on. That's what we want to see. Women in Africa are the backbone of society. Every year I take three teams to the Norway Cup and when, after two weeks away, I ask the player what they most miss about Kenya, they all say "Mama". Not one of them ever mentions their father. That just proves to me how important it is to improve the image of women as role models, because that's how we can change this whole society.'

Three hours later I'm present when the man who introduced women's football to Kenya says goodbye, and tells his audience he is finally leaving the country. He gives a short, emotional speech which, however, doesn't make as much of an impact as it ought to. But then this is Africa. At the end Bob comes over and gives him a presentation vase, then some of the players from the MYSA girls' team come up, and, one after another, shake his hand and place a rose in it. By the end there are twenty-five roses in total, one for each year he spent here in Kenya. It's a very moving gesture, and even Helge has to wipe away a tear.

At last the biggest sports club in Africa has become self-sufficient and it's time for their home-grown managers to take charge of all the sporting activities, including that of their most famous offspring: Mathare United FC.

By now it's really hot but the mixed football team – girls and boys playing together – are about to take on a rival team, after which there'll be music and dancing. All morning there's been music coming from the loudspeakers, save for when it's interrupted for announcements. The atmosphere is great and there's a smile on everybody's face.

Before the music begins I take time to chat with a few of the young people. I come across one group who're clearly getting ready to perform. They immediately ask me which country I live in. When I say Switzerland two boys immediately come over to me with big smiles on their faces and tell me, 'Our music group was in Switzerland in 2009 to play for the United Nations. Geneva was so beautiful.' Astonished to find somebody here who's been to Switzerland, I ask them what they liked most of all. 'Everything was so clean. There was no paper lying on the streets. People even picked up dog poo and put it in plastic bags – just incredible.' The two eighteen-year-olds laugh and shake their heads in astonishment. I can see that if you live in a stinking slum something like that must seem mad indeed.

But they're only getting going. Their eyes light up as they tell me, 'The water in the big lake there was so clean you could see the fish in it. You can't do that at Lake Victoria. And the cars in Geneva were so funny. Once before a performance our group was picked up in a limousine as big as a house. You wouldn't believe it – there was even a table and chairs inside. And a bed.'

The second boy says, 'There was more space in that car than in my house. It really was just like a house on wheels that you could drive around.'

When I ask them if they liked the food in Switzerland they perk up even more and say, 'Well, it was okay but sometimes we were amazed by it. At one stage we were served meat tied together with string and we didn't know what sort of animal it came from and whether or not we were supposed to eat the string. After all, it was served up on the plate.'

The first boy butts in to say, 'But the potato soup was really good, and the meat. It was so soft. I've never had anything like it.'

Both were determined to go back to Switzerland some day. They hoped their band would get a tour booking so they could stay a long time. It's time for the group to perform so I slip back to my seat. By now all the seats are full and I'm amazed to see how many white faces there are in the audience.

The dance group of seven girls, four boys and four drummers take to the stage. There are lots of young people and children standing or sitting round the edge of the pitch, the little ones at the front. Girls of every age are all dressed up beautifully. There are red, yellow and white dresses with ruffles. They've scrubbed up well, done their hair nicely and oiled their faces to make them glisten. You would never know that these were slum-dwellers. Yet again I'm amazed at how they manage to keep themselves so well turned-out given the conditions they live in. A few of the little ones are licking homemade ice lollies which some business-savvy women are selling out of cool boxes.

The drummers start up and the dancers, male and female, start swaying rhythmically if a little shyly. They are all aged between thirteen and eighteen. The girls all seem relatively mature compared to the boys, who cut rather slight figures in comparison. Each girl has a cloth wrapped around her hips and her upper body. The boys dance bare-chested with only a little chain around their necks.

As the rhythm builds the girls match it with the sway of their hips, stamping their feet and singing African songs. Then the boys join in and it gets faster and faster. Gradually the girls drift into the background and it's the boys up front doing a wild, foot-stomping African dance, writhing their slim bodies in every direction so that they resemble human snakes. You can see the ribcages on a few of them, which reminds me uncomfortably of what some of the kids said: that they probably haven't eaten today. Nearly all of them get only one meal a day, usually in the evening. The young boys and girls spinning through the air, sweat dripping down their faces from the heat, is an unforgettable sight. The rhythm gets to me so much that I can hardly keep on my seat.

Their faces beam in recognition of the storm of applause as they finish. The little members of the audience sitting round the pitch clap their hands enthusiastically and the bigger ones whistle in admiration. I could have sat there all night watching them, but the party is gradually coming to an end. Sponsors are handing out cheques, which go straight to the school for whichever child they are subsidising. At the end Bob and Helge give a thank-you speech and gradually people are directed towards the exits. As we too are making our way out, wholly impressed by everything we've seen, I look back and see Helge sitting there on his own, with his head down looking at the vase full of individual roses he was given. Just like Bob he's given his all to this football club and now it's finally time to say goodbye. Things will have to carry on without him, which is how he intended it. He'll come back every year, though, he told me, just like everyone else who falls in love with this country.

FOOTBALL SUPERSTARS IN A DIFFERENT UNIVERSE

Two days after the big party Jecton calls me up and invites me to come and interview some of the players at the club after they've finished training. I can't wait to see if the players will really open up and tell me something of their lives in the short time we'll have.

This time there are no problems getting there and I'm surprised to find their trainer Francis Kimanzi a lot friendlier than last time. As he shakes my hand he tells me he's already started reading my book *The White Masai* and is finding my story quite incredible. I feel very flattered. Then he leads me into a side room and asks me what I'd like to drink while introducing me to the players who've volunteered to talk to me about their lives. Then he leaves us alone.

Sitting in front of me are three young men, all showered and changed after training. They are rather shy and it's not easy to get them talking. And I'm not sure how to get into a conversation with professional footballers, given that I don't know much about football and really want to talk to them about their private lives.

I start out with Antony, the team captain. He's tall and very good-looking. He has a relaxed open manner and soft dark eyes, a full, sensuous mouth with a wisp of a moustache, and a gold chain around his neck. He has an elegant watch on his left wrist, which looks like a piece of jewellery against his dark skin, and there's a slight whiff of male fragrance. I can imagine he has a lot of female fans. I find it a lot harder to believe he still lives near the slums.

I ask him how old he is and he answers me in a clear, strong voice: 'I'm nearly twenty-three and I was brought up in the Mathare slum. Our close neighbours were criminals, drunks and prostitutes. I can't recall even five minutes when I was happy back then. I have five brothers and sisters, two of them already married and three still back home with my parents and grandparents. I live with my girlfriend, but I support my two younger brothers and do my best to save money so that one day I might be able to open a small shop.'

In contrast with all the other people I've spoken to his parents are still together. I mention this to Antony and he is obviously proud of it. 'Yes, they've always set an example for me. Even in the worst of times they did their best to get us through. My father is a car mechanic and still works hard at his job. But things have only really started to get better for us since my mother began selling vegetables. Up until then we had to go to school hungry. The best part of my life back then was that sometimes I would go to the football with my grand-father. I was hooked on the game from an early age. When I was just ten somebody at school told me about MYSA. One of their people came to the school and said, "Don't just hang about after school, get involved in sport. Start up a team, find people ready to do disciplined training and then you can join us: we'll give you a ball, shirts and let you play in one of our leagues. If you show willingness, we'll do the rest."

'That was the turning point for me. I said to myself, "Antony, take on the challenge, get a team together." Before long I was playing in the under-twelve league. It was the start of my career. By the time I was fourteen I was offered the chance to go to Norway to play. That was amazing: being offered the chance of getting into an airplane and flying to Europe. It was a real carrot on a stick for me and I worked really hard. It took four years but I made the grade,' he says with obvious pride.

I ask him how it felt to make his first flight in an aircraft. He laughs and says, 'I was really nervous sitting there on the plane, although not really afraid. A lot of my friends who'd already been to Norway had told me about it. But the reality was much more impressive. I've scarcely words to describe it. I'd never seen such beautiful streets, such big houses and smart cars and such beautiful girls.' The others laugh at his last addition to the list.

I ask him if he'd have liked to stay there and he says, 'Not back then. I was too young. But now I'm working hard at my career. I've been captain for two years. I'll never forget the day we won the cup. We played in front of forty thousand spectators. That was really something. Anyone would love that, and that's why I'd really like to go to a European club. I want to be up there with the elite. Real Madrid, ideally, but there are lots of other great clubs. It's not going to be easy but I'm not giving up my dreams. After all, nobody expected us to win the cup,' he says proudly.

I ask him if he has any other dreams, and he says, 'Obviously I'd like to have a family with lots of children and hope that I can bring them up as well as my parents did with us. And I'd like to give something back to the young people in the slums who haven't had the opportunities I've had. I'm proud to be a role model and would like to do more to change the way of life of people who end up stuck here. Sport is the answer for many of them. Sometimes it's the only way to find the hope and strength to drag yourself out of poverty. You have to train hard, day after day, for no money and without ever knowing if you're going to be offered a paid position with a club. Nowadays there are thousands of good football players in Kenya all dreaming of a professional career. That's why I'm so proud to say I got picked by Mathare United, even if we don't get paid as much as the others and don't have the same sponsorship deals. Mathare is the name of a slum, so it doesn't make for good advertising. Obviously we'd like to bring in more money and then we could do more to bring on young players. But it's okay and we don't have a bad life. We're one big family and Francis Kimanzi isn't just the best coach in Kenya, he's a father figure for us all. He gives us stability, values, teaches us how to cope with success. You don't get anything like that in any other club in Kenya. Lots of the players got to know one another through the MYSA system and have been playing together for ten years or more. You get friendships here you just don't find in other clubs. Everyone here can rely on one another. You can leave your mobile phone or your wallet lying about in the dressing room and nobody will steal it. Nothing like that has ever happened and to me trust like that is worth more than money.'

Joseph, one of the other two, nods at the lad sitting next to him and says, 'I would trust him with every penny I had. But I wouldn't leave him alone with my girlfriend.' I ask if that's because he doesn't trust his girlfriend, but he bounces back with, 'I have one hundred per cent faith in her, but I just don't trust this guy when it comes to women!'

Joseph and the obviously erroneously named Innocent are of comparatively slight build, though Joseph is clearly the bigger-boned. Innocent is a good-looking boy of about nineteen. With his dreadlocks and his well-proportioned, attractive face, I can imagine he's an absolute heartthrob among the Kenyan girls. He's very calm as he tells me that so far his life hasn't been too bad. He is the youngest of eight children and as the baby of the family everybody fussed over him and looked after him. By the age of five he was already playing football with a ball he had made himself out of plastic bags and realised he was quite fast and agile. At seven he was already playing in a MYSA under-ten team.

'And today he comes off the bench for Mathare United to replace me if I get tired,' Joseph teases him. With his frizzy hair sticking out in all directions, a broad nose that rather dominates his face, and a little goatee beard on his chin, Joseph isn't quite as good-looking as his two colleagues. But his laugh is infectious and he laughs quite a lot. He starts telling me his story good-humouredly.

'I'll be twenty-one soon and I've already been playing for Mathare United for some time. I'm the oldest in a family of three brothers and three sisters. There's a lot of pressure when you're the oldest. I had to start looking after my little brothers and sisters quite early on because my mother went out to work. My dad was either out of work or out looking for work. I was young and really needed a role model. Some of our neighbours were luckier and didn't have to muddle through the way I did. Why me? I would ask myself. In the end things went downhill and I joined a gang. By the age of ten I was already drinking and smoking. The older ones forced me. We stole for a living. I gave the food I got at home to my little brothers and sisters. I wasn't good enough to do the stealing myself, but I was fast enough to run off with the loot. The first my parents knew about any of it was when I was arrested and held at a police station overnight.

'They beat me to scare me, but then my mother promised me that if I stopped running around with the gang and started playing football instead she would buy me a proper football shirt. It wasn't easy for her to save enough money but she did it and in the end I got not one but two shirts. That meant I could wear one every day. Other kids who were trying to get a team together for MYSA noticed me and one evening they invited me to join them training. At the end of the night they included my name in the MYSA registration form. I've been playing ever since and I can tell you that MYSA has changed my life completely.

'It was just luck that the other kids invited me to join them. Back then Mathare United didn't exist and the press paid no heed to us. The only people you knew and who knew you were those who lived round and about. Nowadays it's easier for kids to get in on the act.'

I ask Joseph what was the biggest change in his life, and he says, 'From the first day I stopped hanging out with the gang, I started training instead. I got to make new friends and new ambitions. As I'd had to look after my little brothers and sisters, people saw that I could manage responsibility and before long they made me captain. Corinne, I was just eleven years old, playing in the under-twelve league, but that same year I got to fly to Europe to take my team to the Norway Cup. Everything happened so fast I didn't even have time to be scared of flying. I was just too excited. My mother was worried, though, as we would be away in Norway three weeks. She thought I'd never come back, and she insisted I took the number of the people next door who had a telephone, and call her. All the family came to the airport with me, even Grandad. We had to save up to rent a car big enough to take us all,' he says with a grin.

'Norway was like paradise. You could get everything. We got bread, apples, juice, just for breakfast. We stayed with local families who let us eat as much as we wanted. Of course they said, "Joseph, don't eat so much, we're going to have lunch and dinner too." Even during training we got sandwiches, milk or juice rather than just water. The coach was furious, because after just two days we'd all put on weight and got fatter. We could hardly cope with the training.'

I'm crying tears of laughter as he talks about it all. I can imagine they must have thought they were living the dream.

'I was happy but I missed my family. I'd have given anything if they could have experienced life in Norway with me. When I came back at the end of the three weeks my uncle wanted to open my suitcase at the airport, he was so keen to find out what I'd brought him back from Europe. It was crazy, we had no money but the families we'd stayed with had given us T-shirts and socks and things so we had presents for everybody back home.

'Last year I had a great season,' he goes on. 'I came third in the vote for player of the year. I was top scorer with the most goals, and I won three prizes,' he tells us proudly.

'I can imagine your parents are really pleased with you,' I say.

'Yes, they are very proud, but my name's in the papers so much all my relatives think I have to have lots of money, which isn't the case. Now my relatives up country keep expecting me to give them presents. My grandfather rings up every week wanting one thing or another. It's not easy, especially given that I have to support my younger brothers so they can get through school. And I help my mum out financially too now and again. We don't earn lots of money like they do at other clubs. I live with my girlfriend. And now her family are putting pressure on me to marry her. And doing things the traditional way in our society isn't cheap. I have to go and make a formal visit to her family and take lots of my own family members with me. They all have to get together and talk and get to know one another better, and I have to pay for everything, even though they cook the meal. We have to have goat and beef and traditional beer. That all costs a lot of money, and that's just the first meeting.

'My girlfriend's proud of me wanting to do it all the traditional way because that will really earn her a lot of respect from the rest of the family, and for me too. I want my wife to be highly thought of. And then later if we run into difficulties everybody will help, because we're all just part of one big family. Not every woman is lucky enough to find a man who can afford to do everything the traditional way. My girlfriend tries to act as a role model for her younger sister and I have to do the same for my younger brothers. I want them to be able to do things the same way when they get married. I'm just pleased I'm able to make all that possible. It's important to me. But I'm a bit nervous about it all,' he says, blushing.

'This Sunday after the match I'm going on the visit. My family will get there first and I'll come on the bus after the game. I just hope nothing goes wrong and they're all still friends when I get there,' he says with a grin.

Innocent is looking at his watch and says it's time for them to go and do their three hours of voluntary community service. I ask them what they plan to do today and Joseph says: 'Down at the club they split us up into groups and each group does something different every time. Today we're going to see kids in jail, under-eighteens who've been locked up. We try to talk to them, to get them interested in sport, to make clear to them that the life they've been leading is a road to nowhere. I can speak from experience. But now I'm a role model for these kids and that's a great feeling. We sit down with them and they ask us questions. Some of them want to know how I got where I did, to be playing in the top league. I tell them about MYSA, explain how it all works and if any of them are interested I do what I can to help them find a team to play for. Sometimes we take them food or just a football. But some of them don't care. There are boys who don't want to talk to us, won't take any of the food we bring. They just want to be left alone and you can't force them to listen. It's a tough time for these kids. They don't even know if their parents will have them back or if they'll have to go and live in a home. In any case they'll have to go to a special school where they are watched, and do hard work. It's meant to be a punishment.'

I ask the two of them if players from other clubs do voluntary community service. That has them laughing out loud and they tell me, 'No. We're the only club in the Kenyan top flight that does something for their community. Our wages are 50 per cent based on doing this work, but we enjoy helping others. But it can be hard because when they've seen us players in person, they all want to go to a football game and that's not possible. We can't afford it. Sometimes we're allowed to take two fans each. But they enjoy it so much they want to come to the next game too. Even when we're playing away, we set off really early so we can do community service in whatever town we're visiting. Sometimes we'll go into a primary school and give them a training session. The kids really love that. We've only got big thanks to MYSA and we want to give something back on that account,' the pair of them agree emphatically.

They have to go now so I ask them in conclusion what their greatest dreams are. The two of them agree: what they want more than anything else is to play in Europe. 'You know, Corinne, we're doing okay but we're still young. We can't afford to save much money because we have to support all our relatives as well as ourselves. It's important for us to get somewhere while we're still young. We need a contract for several years so we can make a name for ourselves and then later, when we come back to Kenya, we'll have something to build on. We're role models but that means we have to keep up standards. We can't let ourselves sink back into poverty after a few years. That would be disastrous. That's why we keep up good relations with the media and people like you who'll tell people about us in Europe and maybe that way we'll get a chance. That really is our dream.'

I'm not in the slightest surprised that Mathare United, which is made up of young, talented and strong-willed men like these, has twice been nominated for the Nobel Peace Prize.

FINALLY, NAPIRAI MAKES IT TO BARSALOI

After a hectic and busy month in Nairobi I head back home, the moving stories I've been told running through my head. But my conscience is nagging me because I spent such a long time in Kenya without going up to Barsaloi to see my beloved African family. I would love to see them all again after six years – Lketinga, Mama, James and all the others. But I simply couldn't go without my daughter. In letters to them I don't mention my recent time in Kenya because it would cause too many impossible explanations.

But after all the interviews in Nairobi I realise that in any case I will have to go back to sort out some questions I still have. It's also important for me to see the people who shared so many details of their private lives with me for a second time so that I can get a bit more perspective. There may be little things I missed or need to check more thoroughly. I still have a lot of emotions and impressions swirling around in my head and need to sort them out.

It's nice to be back home though and I can appreciate my comfortable existence a lot more than before the trip. Whenever I'm back here I spend all my time dreaming of more adventures, particularly in Africa. But then when I'm away for long periods at a time, no matter how beautiful and amazing everything is, I get homesick. I just remember to keep thanking God that I have the choice. Most people in Switzerland could board a plane and fly off to Africa easily enough and come back a few weeks later. It's not the same the other way round. Only a very few Africans could ever manage to take a holiday in Switzerland, and it certainly wouldn't be easy for them. That is one of the thoughts running through my head as I sit and write down my recollections of my experiences.

I read aloud my stories from the slums to my daughter who sits there in amazement, completely unable to imagine life like that. She knows of course that her African family live an extremely modest existence but at least in comparison with the slums they are relatively free and close to nature. Every story I tell her just increases her interest in Kenya and she asks more and more questions. I'm really pleased by her interest because there's nothing I'd like more than to take my daughter back to show her the country where she was born. I'm certain that it would change a lot of her attitudes and she would understand my own past better. For years now I've been lighting a candle for my African family in a church nearby. I pray for Mama, and of course for Lketinga, Napirai's father, to live long enough for Napirai to be ready to see them. Above all I worry that it might soon be too late for her to get to know her wonderful grandmother.

Then in May I get a letter from my brother-in-law James which changes everything:

Dear Corinne and Napirai,
I really hope and pray you are both well. We praise the Lord that our family is all well and we are content. Stefania, my wife, and I and our children are all in the best of health and Lketinga and his wife and children are happy too.
Once again I want to take the opportunity to thank you and Napirai for everything and say how much we value it all. Please excuse me, Corinne, for not being in touch for so long. You have been supporting us for so long, Corinne, and just by

writing about us you're still doing so every day. It is just great and I pray God to bless your handiwork.

Lketinga's family get the money you send regularly and he thanks you for it. My family also thank you for your contributions you make to us and to Mama. I have no words to express my thanks properly but this is the best I can do.

Dear Corinne and Napirai, it is very important to me to tell you how much we appreciate you. My children and Lketinga's children talk about you often. Some of them know you personally, Corinne, from when you visited with Albert and Klaus when you were writing your book Reunion in Barsaloi. The older members of the family think of you and pray for you daily. Mama tells me always to be sure to send her love to you when I write and whenever you write back, I immediately read it out to her.

Corinne, I am so pleased to tell you that during the last really bad drought which lasted up until a few months ago, we did better than most people in Barsaloi and the rest of the Samburu region. That is simply down to the fact that you have never forgotten your Samburu family and have supported us so generously. I also want to mention our godfather Albert who has also been very generous in helping us.

Dear Corinne, this is a day when I remember a lot of things, particularly going back to those years between 1987 and 1989. Do you remember the day when you went to visit Mama in Loruko, a few kilometres from Barsaloi? Lketinga and I weren't around at the time. But you knew Mama and you and she managed to communicate using sign language and reading each other's lips and eyes. It must have been God's will that brought you to the Leparmorijo family. I remember Lketinga arriving a bit later and the two of you sitting down and discussing your wedding. I am still amazed to this day that you chose to adopt the Samburu culture. You immediately chose to get married like a Samburu woman. You built a manyatta in our corral, a 'white house' we call it because it looks green at first when the outside is all plastered with cow dung and

then when it dries out after a few days it become white. All
the women in our culture getting married for the first time
build a house like that. You did too, which just showed us how
extraordinary you were.

Now I want to tell you about a dream I had a while back,
about a house in the middle of our country. You should know
Barsaloi has changed now. You can buy land and I have
done so. I have a piece of land that nobody can take away
from me. With a lot of hard work, the help of God, and help
from you too, I would like to build this house I dreamt of.
It will be painted white and called Corinne's White House
and it will survive all of us. This house and your books
will remind our children and our grandchildren of you and
the support you have given to the people of Barsaloi in the
Samburu country.

From time to time maybe you will come and visit us and
maybe Napirai one day will make it. The house will be there,
a safe place ready to receive guests. When I am finished the
'White House' will sit there in the middle of our other houses
and all our animals.

Corinne, this is my big dream, because we have to do
something to thank you for all the support you have given us,
and thank God too for being so good to us. I am certain that
one day, sometime in the future, Napirai will come and find a
room waiting for her inside.

PS: I've enclosed photos of all the family with their names
written on each one, so you can see all your African family.

Yours,

James and family.

I'm emotionally bowled over by the letter. Just reading it has made my eyes fill with tears. I feel all the more ashamed that I failed to make it to Barsaloi.

That evening I read Napirai the letter on the telephone and have a lump in my throat as I say the words. I find it hard to control my voice. There's a long pause in which I can hear her breathing on the other end of the line. Then I hear her say the sentence I have waited so long for: 'Mama, you should go back there, I mean, we should go back there! I'm coming with you.'

I can hardly believe it. 'Thank you, Napirai, I'm really pleased you want to take such a brave step. I'm 100 per cent convinced that you'll make them all so happy, and that you'll be happy there too. I wish I was with you right now to put my arms around you and hug you.'

She just laughs and immediately brings me back down to earth, saying, 'I just hope nobody will expect too much from me. After all, as far as I'm concerned, they'll be strangers. I can hardly remember anything from back then. I was so small when you took me away.'

But I'm so happy, all I can say is: 'Don't worry. We'll manage it, just like we've managed everything else.'

Napirai writes: As long as I can remember my mother has been reading me letters from our family in Barsaloi. I've always been fascinated to hear their latest news or to see a photo of my father and the rest of the family. Obviously these days I read the letters myself too. And when we write back I always add a few words in English for my father.

I've often wondered what it's really like in Barsaloi and how things there might have changed. But above all for all these years I've wondered about my father. What will he look like now? What will he be like? What do we have in common? Questions such as these keep running through my head. Obviously my mother has always told me lots about him, told

*me stories about her past. And all this time I've obviously had
my own conception of my family back there in Kenya.*

*Nonetheless I haven't really been that all that intensively
involved in thinking about Africa. The stories and letters have
been all the contact I really needed with my father. But as I've
got older I've become more interested in Africa.*

*I was very moved by the last letter we got from James. I
realised how important the two of us are for the family there. I
feel the time has now come for me to make the journey, to seek
out my roots. This letter has made me realise it's the right thing
for me to do. The time is right. I feel that with both heart and
mind.*

I immediately start planning our trip. First of all, of course, I
need to write to James so that they too can be prepared for us
coming. The letter will then sit at the poste restante desk in
Maralal for several weeks before somebody comes to pick it
up. We can only go in the summer holidays, so I've only got
a couple of months to get everything in order. I can imagine
how excited they'll all be when James tells the family we're
coming to see them. Mama won't believe it until we actually
get out of the car before her eyes in Barsaloi. And what about
Lketinga, Napirai's father? How is he going to react? But I don't
let myself worry about that; I trust God, and Lketinga. After
all, once upon a time he really loved his daughter a lot. If she
cried, he would pick her up and walk up and down with her
for ages, singing Samburu songs to her. I'm certain that seeing
her again after all this time will make him happy.

Pleased and delighted though I am, I can't help being a little
bit worried at the thought of us two women travelling in a
Jeep through the Samburu bushland. So I ask Albert, my publisher, and Klaus the photographer if they will come with us.
Both have already been to Barsaloi with me, met my Samburu
family and got on well with them. They immediately sign up

and I feel enormously relieved, not least because on this trip I shall be responsible for my daughter.

Seeing as Napirai has never even been to Africa before I decide to give her a gradual introduction to Samburu country. First of all we'll head along the old road to Nakuru and spend the night there, before continuing via Nyahururu to Maralal and finally on to Barsaloi.

We start making preparations like crazy but I'm still nervous about how little time we have. I've been waiting in vain for weeks now for a letter back from James. What if it's got lost in the post? Maybe giving them such short notice of our arrival is asking too much. Maybe the timing isn't right? Among the Samburu important events are coordinated with the phases of the moon. I have so many questions whirring round in my head that I can't enjoy the lead-up to our trip. My daughter is concerned too and keeps asking me if I've got a letter yet.

I've also sent word to Father Giuliani. Three weeks before we're due to set off I at least get a reply from him that he'll come to visit us when we get to Barsaloi. Napirai doesn't have long enough holidays for us to go and visit him at the mission down in Sererit, which is several hours away by car. He seems to be looking forward to seeing us.

Then at long last, after writing a second letter and not getting any answer, I receive an email from the new head of the church mission in Barsaloi. He sent it from the post office in Maralal and lets me know briefly that everybody is happy we are coming, particularly the Leparmorijo family. Napirai and I are both hugely relieved.

'Thank you, dear God, for giving us such a comforting sign', I pray. At long last we can start really looking forward properly to our adventure, and there's a spring in our step when we finally board the plane.

We land in Nairobi at the beginning of August. But even as we're waiting in line for immigration control, I start getting butterflies in my stomach. I just hope nothing goes wrong, because after all in Napirai's German passport it gives her place of birth as Samburuland, Kenya, and this is the first time she has been back on Kenyan soil since we fled all those years ago. I just hope we don't have to answer any awkward questions or open up our luggage which is stuffed with presents. Despite all the years that have passed I clearly still have a lingering bad impression of the bureaucrats here. But then it was right here, at this passport control desk, that my attempt to flee Kenya with my baby daughter nearly fell apart. They bombarded me with so many hostile questions that I nearly froze in terror. Now here we are, shuffling gradually towards the desk and my hands are sweating. Napirai, on the other hand, is totally calm. I look for signs of emotion in her face, but she seems absolutely normal.

Eventually we're through and nobody seems even remotely interested in our huge pile of luggage.

Napirai writes: So, here we are on the way at last. That's all I can think about. Here I am sitting in an airplane on the way to Nairobi. In just a few days' time I'll meet my family in Barsaloi. It's crazy! I keep telling myself to calm down. I'm worked up enough just being on a plane. Ever since take-off I've been trying to distract myself, to think of other things and not constantly about what's waiting for me at the other end. Even as we're coming in to land, I find myself getting more and more nervous to the point where I've got stomach cramp. I just wish we'd already landed. Then finally the plane touches down on Kenyan soil, and I suddenly feel a wave of relief wash over me. I can't wait to know what it feels like stepping out of the plane into Kenyan air. I can tell my mother is already very worked up about it. So am I, of course, although unlike her it's

*not passport control I'm worked up about; it's the fact that here
I am in the land of my birth for the first time in twenty years.
I thought the whole thing would have been too much for me,
but somehow I'm managing. In fact, as we drive away from the
airport I feel a great calmness descend on me. It feels good to be
here. My nerves have gone.*

*A driver picks us up and takes us to the hotel. This is the
first time I've been driven along an African road and suddenly
I burst out laughing. Obviously I'm tired from the journey but
I can't help staring out of the windows. Everything is so new to
me and the chaos on the streets is incredible to see. There are all
sorts of people crowding round the car trying to sell us stuff. I
buy some nuts from one boy. I'd like to buy something from all
of them but that's not possible and in any case, this is just my
first day in Kenya.*

*It takes about an hour, with various hold-up in traffic
jams, to get to the hotel. It looks very pleasant and welcoming.
Immediately on entering the lobby I can feel how friendly
everybody is, which is really nice. My mother and I are sharing
a double room and I'm looking forward to getting some rest.
We have a bit of a chat first though as I know how eager she
is to find out my reactions to everything. Both of us are just
happy that we've got here with no problems, and before long
I'm drifting off to sleep.*

After breakfast we set out in two Land Rovers. Even though
there are only four of us I think it's important to take two cars.
The last thing I want is to break down out in the bush somewhere and make a fiasco of my daughter's first trip back to her
roots. She and I take one car while Klaus and Albert go on
ahead of us in the other. Martin, our young driver, is a jolly lad
who keeps us entertained with his relaxed chatter. Yet again
we crawl at a snail's pace through the streets of Nairobi and
then onwards towards Lake Nakuru. The lake is famous for

its pink flamingos, which congregate there in thousands. It's a route I haven't taken before. Several hours later we make a halt at one of the viewpoints looking out over the vast fertile Rift Valley. There are lots of souvenir sellers here and they immediately crowd round us trying to sell hand-carved figurines and other bits and pieces. It's Napirai's first experience of this and she can't resist buying a little box made of soapstone.

We travel onwards through hilly green countryside, passing through little villages along the way. The fields are full of mainly women workers, their feet spread wide apart and their backs bent double as they toil away. I doubt if we Europeans could manage to work like that for hours on end, hoeing, weeding and sewing seeds. The large number of bicycle and motorbike rickshaws is new to me. I didn't notice them six years ago. Now there are rows of them, driven by young men, lined up everywhere waiting for customers. With the traffic getting ever heavier, they are clearly a cheaper and quicker alternative means of getting around, although they are also almost certainly more dangerous. Nearly all the bicycles have wooden boards or plastic seats strapped on to the luggage rack at the rear to provide seating. I can't help wondering where these young people have got the money from to set up a little taxi business, but Martin tells me most of them don't own the motorbikes but are just hired to drive them. 'They nearly all belong to a company,' he says. 'If one of them has managed to get the money together himself, it's usually down to a credit union.' I automatically think back to the women of Jamii Bora, and look forward to going back to see them after the trip to Barsaloi.

We get to our campsite just after midday and sit down to a welcome lunch. We've got a nice, roomy big tent which has everything in it you'd find in a hotel room. This is a much more romantic way to travel than using hotels. At night we can hear the cicadas chirping in the trees and the noises of other animals out there too. There's only a thin canvas wall between us and the natural world.

Next day we set out on a 'game drive', which is what they call the safaris through the national park. We sit and wait in the car while Martin goes to get the tickets. We've already opened the roof so we can stand up and take photographs, and there are primates of all shapes and sizes clambering around: meerkats and the much larger and more aggressive baboons. I'm standing up to take a photograph when all of a sudden an ape barely a few feet away leaps up on to the car and tries to snatch my camera bag. I wave a hand to scare him away but instead he lunges as if to attack me, and I'm the one who's scared. I try to sit down again when another, much bigger baboon jumps up on top of the car and tries to climb in through the roof. Thank goodness, Martin comes back at that minute and they all run off.

We drive through the park past little herds of zebra and buffalo until we come to the edge of Lake Nakuru. Here there are flamingos as far as the eye can see. It's hilarious to see how nearly all their movements seem to be synchronised. One minute they all have their heads in the lake, the next they're all standing staring in the same direction. One minute several thousand of them all take a few steps to the left, the next they all take a few steps to the right. It's as if they've been choreographed. The whole thing is one endless photo shoot. Then to crown the experience a magnificent rainbow comes out, framing the whole picture. Clearly a good omen!

On the way back we come across a small family of rhinoceroses grazing happily in the evening sun and hardly even bothering to look up as we pass.

The next day we start out early, driving past native houses all beautifully painted, some with pictures of giraffes, others decorated with pictures of flamingos or lions or even famous people, such as former president Jomo Kenyatta, or the Nobel Peace Prize winner Wangari Mathai. Some of the houses even have Masai warriors painted on them.

After three hours' drive we reach Nyahururu, the highest city in Kenya, 2,303 metres above sea level, where we are taken to see the spectacular Thompson Waterfall. It's not all that remarkable for us Swiss, though, as we have waterfalls enough back home. What is far more interesting to me is that people here talk to my daughter in Kiswahili, clearly recognising her as at least part Kenyan. But then it's not that far – as the crow flies at least – from here to her Samburu homeland.

But the final stretch of our journey towards Maralal is going to require some patience: from Rumuruti onwards the roads are only dirt tracks and we have just heard that heavy rain a few days ago has turned the red earth into mud. The few cars that use this stretch of road nearly didn't make it through. I know from personal experience what it can be like to get bogged down and stranded. On several occasions I had to spend the night on the bus with nothing to eat or drink. I will never forget the extraordinary experience of being the only white person on the bus, spoiled and looked after by the locals even though I couldn't speak their language. But it turns out we're lucky and there are just some pools of water along the road. When I see the red earth and the savannah landscape I immediately feel as if I'm coming home.

But it's not long before I'm horrified to see that the same thing has happened here as in Namibia. Everywhere landowners have erected fences, closing in vast tracts of land and building huge farmhouses. Six years ago all this land was still open to everyone. It's unbelievable how quickly it has all changed. Where can the semi-nomadic Samburu go with their cattle now? It's only later that I really recognise the problem here: children are forced to graze their little herds of goats or cattle on a few patches of dried grass, while only a few hundred metres away a huge herd of wild buffalo are grazing right alongside the road. That never used to happen before. Buffalo are extremely aggressive. But with the land that used to be open now fenced in, they can no longer wander where they will but have to share the small area of free land with the domestic animals of the locals. And the same thing obviously applies to the other wild animals – elephants, lions and zebras – which makes things much more dangerous for the nomads.

I'm mulling over this rather depressing discovery when suddenly I'm cheered up by the sight of a few Samburu warriors strolling along with their long braided hair. With them are a lot of women in blue and yellow kangas wearing jewellery made of multi-coloured glass beads. That cheers me up a lot as I had feared my daughter might not see any of the traditional clothing because so many children aren't allowed to wear their traditional clothes and jewellery at school. All along the way Napirai is staring out of the window, both interested and amused by what she is seeing.

After five hours' journey along the dirt track we finally reach Maralal, the main town in the Samburu country. We're intending to spend the night in the Maralal Safari Lodge, some distance outside the town, but I can't resist going into the little town centre to see what has changed since my last visit six years ago. Obviously I also want to show Napirai the place where I stopped over so often. For me back then, coming from Barsaloi, Maralal was the start of civilisation. Even now it still reminds me of some Wild West frontier town. Maralal is still the last place in the district where you can get good food and fill up on petrol before setting out for Barsaloi, Lake Turkana or Wamba.

What I really want to do is head for the little tearoom, have a proper chai and triangular mandazi doughnut and soak up the atmosphere, but all the others are tired and dusty, and in any case we've arranged to meet my brother-in-law James at the Safari Lodge. So for now I have to make do with a short drive through town in the car. The centre of Maralal hasn't really changed at all. There are more cars and more people in Western-style clothes but there are still the same rows of little wooden shops, all selling more or less the same sort of stuff.

The more I stare through the dusty windows at the people, the more excited I get. Maybe I'll spot James. He's out there somewhere waiting for us, almost certainly as nervous and excited as I am. He's the only one in the family who has had an education and so has a lot of responsibility as the point of contact between Kenya and Switzerland. My God! It suddenly occurs to me that in a few minutes I shall be introducing my daughter to one of her African blood relatives for the first time since she was barely two years old. I shoot a glance at her and notice a slight flickering in her eyes indicating a certain timorous nervousness. I take her hand and we both suddenly feel very close to one another.

Our vehicles bump along the dirt track up and down a few hills until we get to the simple little lodge. There's nobody in sight, not any other tourists, or any sign of service personnel. Eventually an old Samburu man appears who eventually gets round to serving us drinks. But somehow that too fits in. Nothing has much has changed here since I first came to this lodge twenty-four years ago. Then, just as now, I sat here on this terrace with a few photographs of a handsome Samburu warrior in my hand. I loved that man with all my heart and on his behalf I had sold or given up all I owned back in Switzerland. We had been separated against our will and it was my faith in our indestructible love for one another that had brought me all the way here from Mombasa. I sat there exhausted, drinking a lemonade, staring at the distant mountain range and praying that against all the odds I'd find him again. My strength of will and the strength of our love made it possible, and even to this day I believe it was fate.

And now here I am back again to reintroduce him to his wonderful daughter. Napirai too is very excited about seeing her father and has no idea how she'll react when she does.

There are a few zebra down by the watering hole and some apes playing around behind them, but apart from that everything is very peaceful. Shortly after our arrival a small group of Italian tourists turns up to look at the zebra and then they're gone again.

Before long I hear the sound of a motorbike and realise straight away that it must be James. Napirai and I are still sitting on the terrace when we hear Albert and Klaus welcoming him. We're just about to go and see him, when all of a sudden there he is, a little tubbier than before and clearly a bit tense about the meeting. But he holds out his arms to me, clad in a thick down jacket, and hugs me tight: 'Ay, ay, ay Corinne, you came back!' he exclaims happily. I'm every bit as happy as he is. Then he looks past me at Napirai, laughs loudly and gives her a big hug.

James stands there just looking at her, saying 'Ay, ay, ay, she's grown up. It's not that long ago I was playing with you as a little girl, when I was still at school myself, and now here's a young woman standing in front of me.' He shakes his head as if he still can't believe it. 'And here you are, Corinne, and Albert and Klaus, you've all come back again. I could hardly believe it when I got your letter. We wait for years to see Napirai again and then we get a letter to say you're on your way! The letter was delayed, and I only got it a month before you set off, so I thought it would be better to reply via the priest as he told me the computer would be a lot quicker,' he babbles happily. We all chat and exchange gossip, Napirai clearly struggling with her emotions as she takes James in.

Suddenly James gets serious and says, 'Corinne, Lketinga is here in Maralal too and would like to see his daughter today. There was no way he could wait back home for you to arrive. Is it okay if I go and fetch him?'

'Of course, I didn't think he'd be sitting at home twiddling his thumbs when his daughter was coming to see him,' I tell him.

But one look at Napirai and I can see from the expression on her face that everything is going a bit fast for her.

James takes out his mobile – Maralal is the only place it works – and calls Lketinga, who it would seem also has a mobile phone! They exchange a few sentences and then James is off. I can hardly imagine Lketinga sitting on a motorbike and can't wait for them to get back.

It takes nearly an hour. Napirai can hardly control herself but apart from being here with her, there's nothing for me to do. I only wish I could read her mind.

Outside the zebras are still standing around the watering hole, glancing over at us disinterestedly from time to time. Two of the apes are screeching and squabbling with one another.

I can see Napirai getting more nervous with every minute, but then I'm not exactly calm myself. Then, just as dusk is falling, we hear the motorbike arriving in the quiet night air. A motorbike followed by a car. Surely Lketinga can't own a car, can he? I'm about to go and see, when Napirai grabs me by the arm and holds me back.

Napirai writes: We've been sitting in this lodge for quite a while now, waiting for my father. The surroundings are beautiful and the atmosphere delightful but it seems to me like an eternity passing. I'm not at all sure what will happen when we meet for the first time, whether or not he'll accept me as his daughter. I hope he does. I'm really happy to be here, to be about to meet my father. I keep listening to the distant noise of the traffic in Maralal. Every time I hear the slightest sound, I think, could that be him? It feels as if time has stopped and I'm getting more and more nervous. I'm almost sick to my stomach with the endless waiting.

Then suddenly, after a whole three hours, I hear James's motorbike. I could burst into tears of happiness and excitement, but I manage not to. I just can't believe that in a few seconds I shall see him. I need my mother with me when I meet him for the first time, and thank God, she stays out here on the terrace with me.

A tall, lean figure in a white hat is strolling slowly, elegantly, through the trees towards the lodge. 'Napirai,' I can't hold myself back, 'look, that's your father walking towards us so grandly.'

My own heart is hammering away and I can't think clearly. I feel as if I'm sharing every iota of my daughter's excitement. The only thing I worry about is that it will all go well, and her father will not behave strangely.

Lketinga comes into the room through the terrace door, hesitates for a few moments looking expectantly in our direction. He's got himself specially dressed up for the occasion, I can see that straight away. He's wearing a dark grey jacket that is slightly too large for him but matches his grey-and-white checked trousers perfectly. His white shirt matches his light-coloured, broad-brimmed hat which itself is decorated with orangey brown pearls and small coins. Hanging from his neck is a little wooden flask, also decorated with coloured pearls, which he obviously uses for his snuff. His dark face looks tense at first but as soon as he claps eyes on his daughter it is immediately transformed. I want to rush over to him but he is already making a beeline for his daughter. He passes me, saying in a dark smoky voice, 'Not you, I don't want you, I want my child.' He marches straight over to Napirai, throws his arms round her and hugs her so hard I worry she won't be able to breathe. And then he gives me a warm hug too. He is obviously totally smitten by his daughter and for the next half-hour can't keep his eyes off her, sitting silently and occasionally shaking his head and running his hands over his face. I find it hard too to see just how hard he's struggling to keep his feelings under control. In his culture people keep their emotions to themselves and he's very obviously finding that hard to do right now. Napirai just stands there beaming. I think the tension she had been struggling with too was simply washed away by the great big hug her father gave her, and now any remaining concerns have been shrugged happily aside.

Napirai writes: My heart was hammering in my chest when I caught sight of my father out on the terrace. He looked just

like I imagined and I'm so happy that finally I'm going to meet
him. His faces lights up when he sees me, and he rushes over
towards me. He throws his arms around me and I can fell the
emotion well up in him. All the tension I had been experiencing
evaporates in an instant and I just stand there and savour
the moment. I cannot imagine a better first meeting. I'm
even happier still when I realise he's going to spend the whole
evening with us.

We all sit down around the fireplace, waiting for dinner to be
served, Lketinga between me and his daughter. Every now and
then he takes her hand or puts his arm around her, looks her
in the face and says, 'Yes, my child!'

A friend of James's has come along too. He works in
Maralal, in the government offices, and has a small car. It was
him who brought Lketinga out to the lodge. Gradually, sitting
there around the cosy fire, we all begin to relax. Lketinga
lights a cigarette with his long, thin fingers, laughs and tells
us, 'Yes, I've been here in Maralal for three days, waiting for
you. I wanted it to be me who introduces my child to Barsaloi. I want to show you everything. Why not, I am your father
after all.' Then he puts his arms around her again and squeezes
her. Napirai laughs and I realise that she is enjoying his sheer
spontaneity.

Over dinner he sits opposite me, with his daughter by his
side. He looks better than he did back in 2004, which was the
first time I had seen him since leaving fourteen years earlier.
He seems more relaxed, more at peace with himself. He laughs
at how many pieces of cutlery there are on the table and wants
to know what we're going to eat. Napirai keeps giving him
sidelong glances. James and his friend are telling stories about
the old days, when they came to visit me in hospital after I'd
been taken in – along with Napirai – when I had a recurring
bout of malaria. I glance at my ex-husband and notice he's

looking me straight in the eyes, so intently that it feels as if he's trying to see into my soul. It's almost spooky and I break off eye contact, even though I'd love to know what's going on in his head. I try asking him, but he just shakes his head silently.

Nonetheless I'm happy that Lketinga is here and that the big meeting between father and daughter took place here rather than in Barsaloi. He has a new family with a young new wife and they already have three children. Six years ago he had only just married this young woman a month before I arrived. Despite the fact that they were married they still hadn't spoken to one another, which is not all that unusual among the Samburu, because marriages are arranged by the girl's parents. Most new brides are very shy because they have had to leave their own families at a young age and have often come from far away. Many of them never see their parents again. After they are married the wife is the property of her new husband who has usually paid a hefty price for her. When I was last here I saw his new wife two or three times but never spoke to her. I can't wait to see how much she has changed now that she's the proud mother of three children.

I'm really pleased for Lketinga that things have worked out so well with his third wife. His second wife, Mama Shankayon, is long gone. He sent her back home because she only produced one child. She lives with her blind mother now, helping her. We're going to meet her in Maralal tomorrow as she is very keen to see us and wants to introduce her fourteen-year-old daughter, also called Shankayon, to her half-sister Napirai. Her daughter wants to come out to Barsaloi with us, Lketinga says. It's nice of him to have let her know we're coming as getting in touch with people around here is anything but easy.

When I've finished taking endless photographs of him, he turns to look at me with an amused expression on his face, and says, 'Why do you keep taking photos? I'm an old man now, not as good-looking as I used to be.' The truth is that I'm as fascinated as I ever was with his grace and the way he moves those long, thin fingers. He eats very slowly, and amazingly little. But hardly anything about him now reminds me of the young warrior who would have swallowed half a goat in one evening, sending the bones flying everywhere.

He seems to be looking me up and down the same way. 'You eat a lot,' he says. 'You've really turned into a "Big Mama". Only my child like me,' and he smiles at Napirai. He's not keen on the colour of my hair either. I've gone blonde, but to him it looks white. He's teasing though rather than being malicious, and it really only shows that he's in a good mood.

They leave the lodge late and we agree to meet up the next day at the petrol station, which is one of the few unmistakeable local landmarks. Then we need to go shopping for food to take to Barsaloi, and pick up a few final presents.

At last we fall into bed, exhausted by the long journey and the emotions of the evening. I'm tempted to overwhelm my daughter with questions, but I can see that what she needs right now is rest and calm.

Napirai writes: I really enjoyed our evening in the lodge with James and my father. It was an amazing feeling to sit around the fire with both my parents chatting peacefully, a wholly new experience for me.

Saying goodbye was really hard, but I know that tomorrow we're moving on again and I'll be meeting my half-sister for the first time. I'm really happy as I fall asleep and can't wait for the morning.

We get up with the dawn and all set out together for the prearranged meeting point. I spot my father while we're still in the car, standing at the side of the road with his daughter, my half-sister Shankayon, and her mother.

As soon as we get out of the car a few other curious locals gather round to stare at us. They make me a bit nervous and I'm glad when my mother makes the first move and says hello to everybody. My father is obviously really pleased to see me while Shankayon's mother welcomes me too. I go up to my half-sister and take her by the arm. I can tell she's really pleased to meet us too, and although she's very shy, I immediately like her. I feel really drawn to her, and am suddenly aware how important it is to me to get to know her. Up until today I was an only child, now I have a sister. I can recognise a slight similarity between us and I think she notices it too. The two of us stand there, looking at one another all the time, and every now and then bursting out laughing.

Obviously I've brought a few presents for her, including some earrings and bangles. She's really pleased by them and despite not being able to say much to one another we're already starting to feel close. We all get back into the cars and drive into the centre of town, to do a bit more shopping. I sit in the back alongside my sister. After yet another emotional meeting, I'm starting to appreciate meeting my African family one at a time, so I can take stock of it all. To have met them all at once would have been a bit too much.

We park in front of one of the shops where we want to buy the food and things we'll need, then Lketinga insists on taking Napirai and me on a walkabout around the centre of Maralal. I think I have some idea how proud he is, even though as usual he's put on a stern and serious face. Shankayon follows close behind us, with her mother some distance after her. I've noticed that Lketinga doesn't seem to talk to her much and didn't seem keen on a photo of us all together. Even so, he's given her some money to buy corn meal or maybe something else to eat before she sets off home.

Lots of other people follow us, staring. A few run up to me and my ex-husband has to explain things, which he does in his usual serious, self-confident manner. It would seem we're the main attraction in town today: out here white people still attract attention and Napirai is even more unusual. Lketinga and I look for a woollen blanket for Mama. We haggle with the shopkeepers – something he's still good at – until the price comes down to what he wants to pay, or rather is happy for me to pay. Eventually we do a deal that leaves everybody happy.

The word gets around fast that I've come back with our daughter. We keep coming across women in traditional dress and jewellery or old men who greet me like a long-lost friend, before welcoming Napirai with a hearty handshake and a torrent of words, occasionally reinforced with a good luck spit in the hand. My daughter endures it all remarkably bravely, considering she doesn't know any of them and can't understand a word they say. Even I have difficulty recognising most of them. Lketinga, however, stands there helpfully and patiently reminding me who is who. It's easier for them to remember me as I was the only white face they'd ever seen. For my part, however, I had to get to know hundreds of people. There is also the fact that the Samburus' hard lifestyle means they age faster than Europeans, which makes recognising them more difficult.

We put together the remaining supplies of corn meal, tea powder and chewing tobacco for Mama, making sure we have enough for her to give some to her neighbours. It is traditional that those who have more than others share their good fortune.

Eventually we're all stocked up, the cars full to the roof, and it's time to set off for Barsaloi. Lketinga sits up front next to the driver, giving Martin instructions, while Napirai, Shankayon and I sit in the back. We have a good three hours' driving ahead of us because the cars can't go fast on the rough mountain tracks. It's a testing experience in every way. Even Martin is astounded how bad the road is. He regularly has to engage four-wheel drive, dodge lumps of rock lying in the middle of the track and take care not to send us careering down too steep a slope.

We come across children with herds of goats or cows who wave as we pass in the hope that we'll throw them a sweet. Of course we bought some just for that purpose. The kids run after them excitedly as if it were Christmas. Martin laughs at the way the kids all pile on top of one another trying to get at the sweets. He tells us, 'That was the way I first came across tourists too! We would stand for hours on end outside school waiting for the safari buses. The minute somebody threw a handful of sweets in the air we would all scramble for them. Whoever was fastest was luckiest, because nobody ever shared, unless sometimes we swapped. The one who got most was effectively king!'

He has us laughing again the way he tells this even though we can hardly believe the children wouldn't share their booty. Martin adds shyly, 'It was back then that I made up my mind that I would become a driver with one of the tourist firms – all because of the sweeties!'

We pass a woman with a baby in a cloth on her back and two more in front of her who has to move to the side of the road to let us pass. A bit further on we come across an old man struggling with the slope, carrying a red plastic bag, a stick and a spear. He waves at us, asking for a lift. Lketinga recognises him and asks me if we can make room for him with us in the back. First the old man has to dismantle his long spear to get it inside. Then he spots that there are 'white' people inside and hesitates, but Lketinga tells him we're his family, not ordinary tourists. With a sigh of relief the gaunt old mzee climbs in. All of a sudden the whole vehicle is filled with the smoky smell of a manyatta, reawakening old memories in me and making me long for the moment when I'll sit down once again with Mama.

After more than an hour and a half we reach Opiroi. This little place has really grown. Back in the day there were just a couple of manyattas but today there are wooden houses and a few basic food shops, not to mention a tearoom, a school and a big church. There are people waiting for us and James, who took his motorbike and went on ahead, comes up and tells me that the local chief wants to invite me in for tea. I climb out of the car, but Napirai decides to wait for me. Lketinga strolls over to a shop and buys his daughter a Coca-Cola. I allow myself to be led to the tearoom, although I can't see inside because there's a big jute sack across the door. It is an old tradition that women aren't allowed to see warriors eating or drinking chai. I'm just about to enter the tearoom with the chief when I spot five armed warriors inside about to go off to hunt. I shrink back in horror at offending local custom and instead follow the chief to his private hut. I sit down on a chair while he offers us tea from a Thermos. Then Albert and Klaus come in. The chief thanks us for sending so much money to the mission, which has made it possible for lots of little children to go to school. He tells us he's very happy that thanks to our donations two of his sons have got an education. I'm astonished by this, and moved too. I had no idea that people as far out as this were benefiting from my story. We've still got another two hours' drive ahead of us before we reach Barsaloi.

After a thirty-minute break we set off again. I really am looking forward to seeing Mama soon. Walking over towards the car I notice my daughter trying to have a conversation with a couple of women in traditional dress. She takes a photograph of them and shows them it, which gets them very excited. I'm just pleased to see that she's not afraid of making contact with the locals. We set off, the two women waving goodbye to us as we leave.

Just before we get to the great Barsaloi River, Lketinga turns to us as and with a big smile on his face says, 'Napirai! Napirai, my child, this is my home. I want to show you everything, yes, everything.' The car takes us over the broad sandy riverbed and gradually up the other side. I can see the white mission building from afar, then all the wooden houses and a few manyattas between them, as ever surrounded by thorn fencing. We park under the same tree where fourteen years ago, last time I was here, Lketinga welcomed me back and put his arms around me for the first time since I fled from him. That really brought the tears to my eyes.

I'm still recalling that event as he steps out and opens the car door for his daughter. Immediately there are children all round us, particularly Napirai. The grown-ups take their time coming over, then a few of them call to me, 'Mama Napirai, supa, serian a ge? Hello, how are you?' A few of them shake my hand so long and hard I think my arm's about to fall off. Others rattle their necklaces in a sign of welcome and hold out their hands, in particular to my daughter, who just stands there in amazement, as people all around her call out, 'Supa, serian a ge, garai? Hello, how are you, my child?' Napirai returns their greeting with a shy smile, giving me a sideways look as she hasn't really got a clue what's going on.

Napirai writes: At long last we're on the way to Barsaloi! I'm pleased Shankayon is coming with us. Her presence helps me keep calm. I had no idea how tough the journey was going to be. I kept having to pull myself together to stop falling asleep: the last thing I want is to fall asleep as we get to Barsaloi. The closer we get though, the more my mother gets excited and keeps telling me stories from the old days, pointing out places where such and such a thing happened.

I can hear people's voices even before we reach Barsaloi, particularly children's voices. I can feel myself starting to get nervous again. How will they react to me? I just hope for the best as we drive into the centre of the village. There are lots of women and children already waiting for us. When we get out they all rush up to my mother, saying they can't believe she has come back. They all seem to remember her, which I find incredible.

Then they all want to meet me, and I'm shaking one hand after another. It's really nice that all these people I've never met before are so happy just to see us. It's all a bit embarrassing.

But what I like most are all the village children who rush up to us laughing. Before long I have a little boy or girl holding on

*to my hands. I'm just trying to take stock of where I am, but I
have children clambering all over me.*

*The village is bigger than I had imagined, the houses a
bit like Maralal, although it's not so busy here. After all these
years, here I am finally in Barsaloi. I can't believe it. It seems
like a dream.*

In the wake of the women the first old men now come over
to us and I recognise Papa Saguna, Lketinga's older brother,
shuffling towards us. As always he has a very serious look on
his face, but I can tell he is glad to see us as he holds out his
hand to me. He has aged enormously and his eyes have taken
on a pale blue translucence, almost certainly due to cataracts.
Like Lketinga he is very slim and still wears mostly traditional
dress. Instead of trousers he is wearing a loincloth and has
white plastic sandals on his feet. He has a thin, red-striped
blanket over a red T-shirt. Sadly I can only exchange a few
words with him as he speaks only maa and I have forgotten
nearly all of the little I once learned. He holds out a hand to
Napirai too, laughing so loud that he shows off a row of perfect
white teeth. For a brief moment his eyes light up and he says,
'Supa, Napirai, serian?' Everybody greets one another in the
same formulaic way. He's not the type to throw his arms round
people, but the warmth in his greeting is real enough.

James invites us into the corral to meet the rest of the
family. But Lketinga wants to show us round his shop, which
he has called 'Inter White Masai'. It's quite dark inside and I
can hardly make out what he has for sale apart from second-
hand clothing, some washing powder and a few bars of soap.
What light there is, is partly blocked by the horde of village
children standing in the doorway watching us.

Lketinga's wife squeezes past us and goes to the door
to fetch two of her children. She wears the traditional neck
ornaments and looks very pretty. I guess she must be in her

mid-twenties. She's very shy but when it comes to handing out the gifts later it's clear that she doesn't dislike me. After all, her three children, all of them born within the last six years, are also half-brothers and -sisters to Napirai.

We leave the shop and enter the corral, which is rather big now, with a little toilet hut complete with pump flush loo to one side along with a few manyatta-style huts for the younger goats. Hens and chickens are scrabbling around in the grey dust. James takes us over to his house where his wife Stefania is waiting for us and immediately embraces me and then hugs Napirai. She is a very pretty woman and just right for James. They already have five children and, judging from her shape, number six is on the way. But people don't talk about things like that here.

James's older children charge straight at Napirai and me, obviously delighted to see us. Only the youngest, a girl of about a year or so, cries at the sight of our light-coloured faces. Stefania takes her off to somewhere she can't see us to calm her down. Her older sister, however, comes over to Napirai and takes her by the arm.

I'm still trying to find out which children are James's and which Lketinga's when I hear a sob behind me. It's Lketinga's sister. I used to really like her, even if she was often as serious and sad-looking as her oldest brother. Now here she is, coming over to me and throwing herself into my arms, sobbing. She presses her head against my neck, wetting it with her tears. Her entire body is shaking and I do what I can to try to calm her down. I'm incredibly touched and find it hard to hold back the tears myself. Lketinga merely looks the other way, but James laughs, with a hint of embarrassment, for displays of emotion are frowned upon. All I hear from his sister is, 'Corinne, Corinne,' and then she breaks free and goes over to Napirai, only to repeat the whole scene. She sobs in her arms while Napirai strokes her naked back, trying to calm her down, and looks at me asking what to do.

Napirai writes: I always wanted our meeting with the relatives to be happy and friendly. But I had never expected our arrival to be met with such emotion. I'm completely overwhelmed and our reception in Barsaloi is one of those things that will remain with me all my life.

I immediately get on well with Stefania and the rest of the family. I can speak to her in English and tell her how exciting it all is for me. I get on particularly well with James's children, who are all very good-natured and jolly. His youngest son Diego seems to get on with me straight away. Every chance he can, he climbs on to my lap. I've even taken to heart my three little half-brothers and -sisters. It's great that there are so many children because they're so easy to get on with.

So many children follow us around all the time that we have to close the door to James's house in their faces so we can look round without being surrounded by them. It's not very large inside, but it's been well decorated and I feel quite at home. I'm sitting on the couch with my mother and father, James, his older brother and a couple of the kids. Stefania has made chai for us all, so we just sit there chatting together drinking our tea. My mother starts telling stories about the old days again and Lketinga and James laugh. I think they all remember her stories too.

After tea with James we all go back out to the village square where our cars are parked. We want to fetch the rice and the rest of the food we bought in Maralal for Stefania.

By now even more people have gathered to say hello to us. Some of the women have tears in their eyes when they see us. They all keep repeating the same phrase, which I don't understand. There are crowds of men and women around my mother, greeting her and asking her questions. This goes on for some time and I'm glad James can at least translate some of it for me so I can get a grip on a few sentences and even answer a few questions myself.

After we've put away all the food we brought, James takes us quietly over to Mama's manyatta. I just hope I don't blub when I see her again. The corral has changed a lot since my last visit. Mama's manyatta used to be right next to James's stone-built house, but now instead James leads us across the sandy soil of the central part of the corral to a square, red, simple clay-built house. James leads our little party with some twenty kids trailing in our wake and before long I spot Mama, sitting upright and elegantly as always on the ground outside her house. She has a brightly coloured shawl around her neck, as always decorated with the traditional ornaments, but hardly covering her large naked bosom. She spots me too and begins clapping her hands, smiling and chanting, 'Supa, Corinne. Corinen garai, my child.' I kneel down in front of her and we put our arms around one another and touch our foreheads together. Just the smell of the manyatta emanating from her comforts me. All the time she keeps saying, 'Corinne, asche oleng, Enkai, thank you, dear God.' She pulls my head down towards her, looks me in the face and kisses me on both cheeks. I'm amazed how strong she still is. She still looks great and hardly changed at all since last time I was here. Mama is one of those people who just doesn't get any older. She takes a good look at me again, laughs and asks me again how I am. Then comes the question I've been waiting for, 'Core Napirai? Where's Napirai?'

I stand up and let my daughter take my place. She was standing a bit back with her father and the children, watching Mama and me. Now she bows down to Mama and immediately those strong dark hands take hold of her and pull her down to be kissed over and over again. For minutes on end Mama holds my daughter's head in her hands as she beams at her granddaughter. We can tell just how happy she is by all her clapping and laughing. I've never seen her so happy.

She asks James something and listens attentively to his

answer before welcoming Lketinga with a slap on the back and exchanging a few sentences with him in maa. Then she looks up at us again and says, 'Corinne, Corinne, Napirai, Napirai', and holds out her hands towards us. We kneel down in front of her again and share her pleasure as she holds on to me with one hand and her granddaughter with the other. This time her happiness spills over and I can't hold back the tears any more. Napirai looks over at me and says with a laugh, 'Mama, she's way cool!'

Napirai writes: I've only been in Barsaloi a little time but already I've seen and experienced so many new things that I've hardly had time to take it all in, sit down and think about it. But maybe that's for the best. To be honest, I can't think about anything other than just making the most of every moment we're here. The trouble is that I can't stay that long and I think it'll all really only sink in when I'm back home.

I'd looked forward so long to meeting my grandmother and it's really great that she has regained sight in one eye. I would have loved to spend time with her, just me and my mother and her, but that isn't possible. It seems people here do everything all together and so even the first time I go to meet my 'Gogo', my grandmother, there's a whole troop following me.

As we approach her hut I spot her sitting on the ground outside the door. I can see my mother is getting very emotional because for a moment everything goes quiet. My mother is first to greet her and I can tell how pleased they are to see one another. I suddenly understand how strong my mother's emotional tie to this woman is.

Then suddenly I hear my name being called out. I'm not really sure what I'm supposed to do or say so I just wait there. Then she takes my hands and says something to me. I don't understand but I get the gist. I can tell she's very moved to see me after such a long time. It's very emotional for me too and I

really have to pull myself together as I don't want to break into
tears.

My grandmother is very old and nobody knew if she would
live long enough for us to meet. Now I am really pleased that
we have done.

Looking closely at her face, she doesn't really seem as old as
she is. The main impression she makes on me is of being strong
and very aware, and what is most impressive is the feeling of
calm and contentment she radiates, which is just incredible.

I notice the stick by Mama's side and realise she must have
trouble walking. James confirms this. 'She can't really get up
or walk any more, so she just sits here. But she's been better
since her eye operation last year. They were able to save the eye
that had gone almost totally blind and now at least she can see
again with one eye. We were going to repeat the operation on
the other eye, but she says one is enough.'

Lketinga hands us an empty carrier bag so we can sit down
on it next to Mama. His sister plonks herself down on the
greyish-reddish dirt next to me. She still has a sad look on
her face and is starting to sob again, but Mama turns a stern
gaze on her and says, 'What are you crying for? Pull yourself
together. It's really nice that she's here, not something to cry
about!' Lketinga laughs as James translates for us. It's always
the same here: the only time you're supposed to cry is for the
dead. It's not acceptable at any other time. I put my arm around
her sympathetically and try to calm her down. Eventually the
sobbing dies down, and Mama and I can have a conversation,
thanks to James patiently translating for us.

All the children clustered round us are eventually too much
for Mama and she starts asking them all what they think
they're doing here. James and Lketinga shoo some of the ones
that don't belong to the family away, and they do as they're told
and hurry off. But it's time now for us to set up our camp for

the night before it gets dark, so we take our leave and promise to come back tomorrow for tea. I need Napirai to spend some time inside a manyatta-style dwelling so she can know what it's like and understand how she spent her first year of life with me here. Mama says thanks to us again with another 'Asche oleng, asante sana,' as we take our leave for the day.

We leave the corral and it quickly fills with goats returning from pasture. That's always the best part of the day. But today we don't have time to sit back and enjoy it. We have to get on with setting up our own camp. In an hour's time it'll be pitch black as there's still no electricity in Barsaloi. Looking at the hordes of children still clustered around us I ask James if now would be a good time to hand out the sweets we've brought. 'Yes,' he says, 'that's a good idea. That'll make them happy and they'll all go home.' I give Lketinga and James a handful of sweets each and hand out some myself. Immediately it's chaotic as other kids rush over from their own huts as nobody wants to end up empty-handed. James the schoolteacher intervenes and gets them all to line up or else there won't be any more. That works fine until they start to notice that the bags are nearly empty. Then the little hands all reach out towards us and before long the queue has collapsed. Despite the huge number of sweets we brought there aren't enough for all. Some of the littlest kids can't believe they didn't get any and I'm trying to work out where on earth we can get more from, but James just laughs and says, 'No problem, Corinne. You could never have enough for all of them. You've no idea how many kids there are in Barsaloi nowadays.'

James takes us over to the mission while Lketinga and Papa Saguna, who has joined our little group unobtrusively, wait for the rest of the goats. One of them is going to end up as our evening meal and the two of them want to choose which. We would have been fine with spaghetti but tradition dictates that honoured guests have to be served a slaughtered goat as a sign of welcome.

The new Colombian missionary gives us a hearty greeting

and offers us rooms for the night in the mission house. Napirai and I are glad to accept. We have tents with us but it's bound to be quieter and more comfortable in a house with showers and proper toilets. Albert is the only one determined to put up his tent roof over the Land Rover. The drivers in any case sleep in the open to guard the vehicles. We sit in the mission, which I know from the old days, and drink a cup of coffee while they set up the tent. The Colombia missionary is very different to old Father Giuliani. He's very chatty and ready to help, but not exactly the blue sky thinker and tireless old warrior that Giuliani is. I look forward to seeing him tomorrow.

By now it has got completely dark. All of a sudden Lketinga is standing there in the doorway. He nods coolly to the missionary and then invites us over to James's house, where dinner is served. We haven't had to watch the ceremony of slaughtering the goat, which both Napirai and my publisher Albert are relieved to hear. We take out our torches and follow Lketinga, who skips light-footedly on ahead of us.

James's house is still the same one he lived in six years ago, but he has changed it inside. It is a simple concrete structure with a corrugated iron roof and looks a bit like a barracks. There are three rooms: a kitchen with pots and pans and plates and a gas cooker, a bedroom, which he shares with Stefania and the two youngest children, and a large living room. The older children sleep in a separate 'kids' house' just next to the main one. Later on they proudly show us round their own little domain, which I can tell is pretty lively at times.

Now here we are all sitting around the living room, which has two sofas, some bookshelves, a few chairs and a little table. One of the walls has an artistic mural showing landscape scenes and animals. James tells us proudly it's the work of one of his former pupils.

Our two drivers are invited in to share dinner. They know nothing of my story or why we're even here. Stefania serves up wonderful rice with goat meat, vegetables and a separate plate with pieces of grilled meat. All the others eat more than we four Europeans, who find freshly slaughtered goat meat a bit tough, but I save our honour by taking second helpings. After dinner, Martin, our driver, asks how we know this family in Barsaloi. Everybody bursts out laughing. I start to tell him my White Masai story, with James butting in from time to time to explain something. Lketinga just sits there listening carefully. Only now and again does he nod his head or smile or confirm our version of events with a simple 'Yes.' The drivers, however, are dumbstruck. They thought we had just booked a private safari through the Samburu country and had dropped in to visit a family we knew. They can hardly believe that Lketinga was my husband and that I lived here for several years cut off from civilisation. They thought Klaus and I were a couple, that we had adopted Napirai and had just discovered the identity of her real father, and that Albert was her father-in-law. We all fall about laughing at how wrong they'd got it. It takes a while for me to tell the rest of my story, though I leave out some of the more difficult bits for the sake of not damaging the good mood.

Eventually it's time for us to go. It's been a long, tiring and emotional day. Lketinga accompanies us to the mission door.

Shortly after I find myself lying there in bed, listening to the distant murmurings of the villagers in their manyattas. All of them can hear every word their neighbours say. I can hear the laughing voices of children telling one another stories. Now and then I hear the sound of bells around the necks of the goats, or a dog barking. Napirai is dead to all of it. She fell fast asleep straight away. I wonder about how the day has been for her. At least none of it seems to have stopped her getting a sound night's sleep. I give thanks for a happy reunion, and most of all for the fact that, despite her advanced age, we were able to share it with Mama too.

The next day we're about to set off for a walk round Barsaloi when a car dashes past us, then abruptly comes to a halt, and with a big grin on his face, out jumps Father Giuliani. Just as twenty years ago, he's wearing shorts, a striped T-shirt and his legendary flip-flops. He immediately starts out talking Italian as he throws his arms around me and Albert as if we were old, long-lost friends. Straight away he asks me about Napirai, who's still sleeping off the experiences of the day before. He's only just arrived but already he suggests that we go for a picnic on the dried-up Barsaloi riverbed. He has three guests from Italy with him and they've brought some food. Lketinga and James are happy to agree, as long as they can bring some food along too. Stefania has cooked two big pots full of rice and goat meat in a tasty sauce and has baked some chapattis to go with it. Meanwhile we go back to the mission and have a cup of coffee while we wait for Napirai to get ready.

As soon as she appears Giuliani starts telling her at length all her mother went through here and that she's been here before to visit him when she was just a tiny baby. Clearly my daughter can hardly keep herself from laughing aloud at the pastor's bubbly, effervescent personality. He's a real live wire and as full of energy as ever, even though he must be over seventy years old now.

Eventually everything is ready and we set off. Stefania has packed up our lunch in several pots which we have to position carefully in the car so they don't all spill as we drive along the bumpy track. Napirai's little half-brother Lodunu is determined to come with us, as is Diego, James's younger son. Ever since we arrived the two of them have clung to Napirai and idolised her. I think all the children fussing around her has made it a lot easier for her to get comfortable with her African family.

We've been driving for a fair bit along the dried-up riverbed when James asks just where exactly we're headed for. It seems nobody knows exactly, except for Lketinga who's sitting up front next to the driver. With that deep dark voice of his, he says simply, 'I know. Go, go!' pointing straight ahead. There's a lot of activity as usual along the riverbed. A few women and one or two children are digging waterholes in the sand. Then they fill their cups with the precious water filtered by the sand and pour them into canisters. We come across several herds of goats being driven along the riverbed by children from the village. As soon as the goats smell the water, they're unstoppable and charge past us bleating loudly. As most of the goats are white, I have no idea how the children manage to sort out whose are whose afterwards.

By the river's edge stand succulent green acacias, a clear indicator by their condition that it rained heavily last month. We drive on and on and gradually we start to wonder where on earth Lketinga is taking us. The riverbed here meanders broad and wide across the landscape, across stony reaches here and there or occasionally past some red shrub or other in blossom. From time to time we send tribes of apes leaping and screeching up into the trees, or send camels scurrying away from the cars in that funny, awkward way they have of running.

Suddenly, in the middle of nowhere, Lketinga points to a big tree on the bank and says we've arrived. It's nice enough, I think to myself, but not exactly overwhelming. He opens the car door for Napirai and me. 'Come,' he says, 'only one minute!' He takes me by the hand and pulls me through the rough grass up a little hillock. And suddenly the view takes my breath away: we're standing next to a little lake. I look at Lketinga in amazement. He laughs and says, 'Yes, I know everything here.'

By now the others have joined us and they're all equally surprised, even Giuliani who's lived around here for forty years but never come across this little lake. Even James didn't know about it. 'Yes, I know,' says Lketinga. 'The only people who know about this lake are those who're out every day with the animals and have managed to walk this far. Boys who've only been to school don't know anything about their own country,' he says teasingly to James. He never brought me here before either. The little lake shines in the sun and on the opposite bank two naked warriors are bathing and washing their kangas. It could be a scene from the Bible.

The pots full of food have been laid out on a flat-topped tree root and Giuliani is dragging a folding table and chairs over to lay out the bananas, papayas and mangos he's grown himself. They're delicious, the flavour is so much more intense than anything we can buy in a supermarket. We've also got salami, ham and cheese as well as the delicious dish made by Stefania. Back in the days when I lived here we didn't dare dream of a treat like this.

The two young boys are climbing around the trees like monkeys. Back in Switzerland people are always telling two- to three-year-olds to be careful and nobody would let them climb trees on their own. Lketina's son Lodunu is particularly wild, extremely agile and good-looking. He has three strings of glass beads around his neck, the animal teeth hanging from them, and his stomach is covered with fine scars. He is incredibly proud of them and his equally proud father explains, 'He was determined to have them, and didn't even cry, even though they shed blood. One of these days he'll be a great warrior.' He pulls the kid over and hugs him. He also wants Napirai to sit next to him. Everything he does is so gentle, even when he removes a leaf from her hair. They are so trusting and natural together, it is hard to believe we only arrived yesterday.

Eventually we get to the end of the meal and Father Giuliani is still telling tales of the old days. A couple of old men come up to us looking curiously at our plates, and fairly obviously hungrily. Lketinga gets up, and goes over to offer them something to eat. Then he goes back to his daughter and I watch the two of them chatting and laughing, Napirai with her little half-brother on her lap.

Giuliani is obviously delighted to see us and is chatting away and joking with Albert. The two of them are recalling the last time we came when we went to Sererit. The time flies by and before long we have to be getting back; Giuliani and his guests have a lot further to go. I also want to go back to see Mama, as she's going to be wondering why we haven't come round for tea. There are also the gifts we brought to be handed out; so far all we've distributed was the food.

We bid Giuliani a hearty farewell and promise him that next time we come we'll also visit him in Sererit. As they drive off, he calls out to me, 'Corinne, next time you come I'll put your bed out under the stars so you can listen to the lions roar in the night.'

I laugh and say, 'Then I'll definitely come.'

By late afternoon we're back in Barsaloi. First we have to take the empty pots back to Stefania and thank her for the delicious meal. Then Napirai and I go over to Mama's house. We take with us the beautiful fluffy blue blanket we bought for her in Maralal. I announce our arrival in the traditional way by saying 'Godie,' outside the door. She replies, 'Karibu.' Welcome.

This clay house isn't as low as a manyatta so we don't have to crouch as much. Mama is sitting on the right of the doorway on a cowhide. In front of her is the hearth, marked out by three big stones, and she has a mosquito net hanging over her. We scramble over the gently smoking hearth and sit down on another cowhide. Mama asks us if we want chai and of course we say we do. Her tea is always the best. She calls out and the Papa Saguna's youngest daughter comes in, a pretty, jovial girl, who must be wearing several kilos of red jewellery around her neck. She's nothing like as shy as Saguna was at her age. She has, in any case, a different mother. Mama tells her to light the fire and the girl blows on the embers and places a couple of thin twigs on top. Immediately the air is filled with acrid smoke, which keeps up until finally a little flame appears. Napirai almost chokes to death. I remember being the same the first time I visited Mama in her manyatta some twenty years ago. Even now we both have tears running down our cheeks and my daughter looks ready to make a run for the door. It's not helped by the severed goat's head sitting on a tin box directly opposite her, left over from last night's dinner.

Meanwhile Lketinga's sister has joined us, bringing some goat's milk in a gourd. Mama takes one of the three dented metal pots sitting next to the hearth and puts exactly the right amount of water into it before putting it on the fire which by now is burning nicely. Then she adds some powdered tea. The sister wants to talk to us but without somebody to translate it's impossible. I get angry with myself for having learnt so very little of the maa language. But even without words there is an atmosphere of affection and mutual trust in the little room.

The water has come to the boil and Napirai and I are sweating from the heat given off. Mama tips some sugar from a full jar into the pot and pours some milk from the gourd in. That's the chai done and to me it tastes absolutely delicious, although my daughter doesn't seem to be quite so taken by the sweetness mixed with the unique local flavours of smoke and goat. She can only get a couple of sips down, even though Mama keeps on at her, 'Napirai, tamada, tamada'. Drink, drink, she says, clapping her hands. At that moment Lketinga appears in the doorway, comes in and sits down next to us. Seeing that our daughter is having a few problems with the chai he says to her, 'No problem, my child,' and empties the cup himself. Even so, Napirai can't take being in the hut much longer not least because she gets claustrophobic. She disappears out the door into the sunlight and fresh air.

Napirai writes: My granny is really happy to see us again when we visit her a second time. We sit down in her hut with her. Somehow I had thought it would be bigger. I hadn't realised the hearth would take up so much room. She offers us chai and although I normally like tea, in this heat I would rather have had a glass of water. But I still accept the offer with thanks.

My father arrives and the four of us sit there in the hut

drinking tea. It's really nice us all being together like this but after a while the heat and the smoke are too much for me and I have to go outside. I stand there hoping that my sudden exit hasn't offended anybody but I really couldn't take it any more.

With the best will in the world I can't understand how my mother managed back in the old days. But I have to admit the experience is interesting. When my mother comes out a little later she looks at me and has to laugh. I reckon she knew how I was going to react. She understands that the mixture of sweet chai, smoke and heat is something you have to get used to. She tells me she's pleased I came along to take tea with her and Mama. I know it's something she always wanted to see.

We head back to James's house where the rest of the family have got together. Albert and Klaus are already there so we reckon it's a good opportunity to hand over our presents. I've mainly brought clothes: children's things, skirts and shawls for the women, polo shirts, shirts and hats for the men. Everybody is pleased with their presents, even Lketinga's wife, who seems pleased with a skirt. Nobody grabs for anything, even the children, who sit and wait patiently, happy to get a T-shirt or a little skirt. The real hit among the boys is the World Cup football, which Albert has brought them. Within minutes they're out kicking it around the village square.

Now there are presents for us too. Stefania gives Napirai a broad, brightly coloured necklace she made herself. She gets a headdress too, the sort worn by unmarried girls. It's a sort of band that goes round the forehead, decorated with glass beads and with two little chains that dangle down the cheeks. Then she is also given a white shawl embroidered and decorated with beads to wear around her shoulders. She looks just like a Samburu girl! Her father is clearly so proud and tweaks it a bit here and there, though I can see that my oh-so-modern daughter finds it all a bit weird. There's also a shawl for me,

a little smaller, while Albert and Klaus get leather belts decorated with beads. We're all very moved by the time and effort
they've put into making the gifts for us.

Later on we look through photo albums and even find some
old pictures of me with Napirai as a baby. Just looking at them
makes me realise how mad those days were and how much my
life has changed since then. I regret none of it, but there's no
way I could live like that now.

Suddenly we hear the bleating of goats, the signal that the
herds are coming back, which is something we really want to
see today. The newborns remain behind in a little hut while
their mothers go out to graze. But now they know their
mummies are coming home and go crazy with impatience.
Mama is now sitting outside her hut again. also waiting to see
the herds come home. A few of the children, already wearing
their new clothes, are playing with waiting kid goats. Lketinga's
sister is already with her gourd to milk the goats. She seems
to be in a good mood today with her pretty smile on display.

Then the moment arrives. The white and speckled goats
stream through the gates of the corral. The noise is phenom-
enal. The baby goats are released to seek out their mothers.
Albert-Tonic, James's oldest son, has been out with the goats
all day, as this is the school holidays. The eleven-year-old
doesn't seem in the slightest tired, even though it must be hard
work for a schoolboy. My publisher Albert is particularly glad
to see him. For the past couple of years he has been sponsor-
ing his godchild and hopes that one day he might even go to
college. He has set up a savings account for him.

Papa Saguna's daughter and Saruni, James's daughter, sit
down to milk the goats. They ask Napirai and me if we want
to help. We have a go but it's not very successful, which gets a
laugh from everyone.

The animals don't produce much milk in any case, even
though it's an important element in the diet here. We stand
around a while watching all the goings-on. It's fun to watch the
little children playing with the baby goats. There are virtually

no toys here in Barsaloi but even so, or perhaps as a result, the children seem full of the joys of life.

Shortly before dark we all go back to the mission buildings. On the way we notice how busy things are in all the manyattas. There's the smell of fires and food in the air. We don't want to impose too much on Stefania to make all our meals so tonight Albert and I are going to cook up spaghetti on the gas stove in the mission, and invite the missionary. Later that evening we accompany our meal with a glass of red wine in the open air, under the twinkling of millions of stars.

The next morning we stroll up to the corral early. The goats haven't left for the day yet and all you can hear is bleating. Papa Saguna is sitting on a tree stump in the sunshine in the middle of the herd cleaning his teeth with a piece of wood. It's all very relaxed at this hour of the morning. Eventually James mentions that they normally go to a Samburu market on a Saturday to sell things they have in the shop here. People come to the market from all around so there's a lot of business to be done. But today they're planning to stay at home because we're here.

We simply can't allow that, not least because the market has only been going six months. James is pleased we're interested and within no time they've packed up a load of *kangas* and jewellery from the shop and loaded them into our car. Lketinga is sorry he doesn't have enough of a choice of second-hand clothing. He takes Napirai into the shop and before long she comes out wearing a long black skirt which really suits her. I'm guessing the real issue here is that Lketinga doesn't want his daughter going to a traditional market wearing jeans. Women in trousers are rare enough here.

Lketinga, James and Stefania and the two little boys Lodunu and Diego get into our car and off we go through the dusty red savannah. If it weren't for the tyre tracks it would hardly be recognisable as a road at all. There are no signposts. It takes us about half an hour to get there. I'm amazed to see how many people there are. Most of them have come on foot. But there are also car owners who've come specially to offer a matatu communal taxi service bringing buyers – and sellers with all their wares – to the market. Most of the others have brought their wares on the backs of donkeys.

The market place is in the midst of the steppes at the foot of a mountain range. The stalls look a bit like manyattas but they're built from the thorn-free cacti that grow round about. These are incredible plants: you can just pull one from the ground and plant it somewhere else and it will continue to grow just as well. They put branches across between two cacti supported on the long narrow leaves and then cover them with twigs and usually a sheet of plastic to provide shelter from the hot sun, and a screen against nosy onlookers.

James and Stefania busy themselves spreading their plastic sheeting over their stall but I can't get over just how many traditionally dressed girls and warriors there are here. It feels like twenty years ago. The only signs of the changes that have occurred almost everywhere else are the few cars, and a few visitors who, like James, are dressed in modern clothing.

Stefania's best sellers are the *kangas* and the multi-coloured beading local women use as jewellery. Most of her customers are young warriors buying presents for their girlfriends. The more jewellery a young woman wears around her neck, the more she attracts attention and the higher the price she will fetch as a bride. The one thing that is taboo is for her to marry her boyfriends. Her father will choose her husband and obviously he will pick someone with a good reputation, but also able to pay a high price. That's the way it always used to be done and it seems in that respect nothing has changed.

As usual Napirai is busy entertaining her little half-brother and his cousin Diego. Lketinga and I take a walk around the market. Here there's a group of women sitting under a shady acacia tree, over there a group of young warriors all splendidly attired are standing around talking. Not far away from them is a group of richly bejewelled young women. It looks a bit like a market for prospective brides.

A little bit further on they are slaughtering goats, and building fires to roast them on for sale. Every now and then older people come up to me and say, 'Supa, Mama Napirai, serian?' More than once Lketinga has to explain that I'm only here on a visit.

It's all very self-contained and after a while it feels a bit awkward to be a white person here. But I can't get enough of the wonderful colours and the people all dressed in such traditional fashion. I'm particularly amused by the new fashion for headwear: the most popular would seem to be the sort of plastic tulips we get at markets back home, except that here two or three of them are tied together and woven into a hairdo. I notice though that none of the men have painted their faces. In his warrior days Lketinga had decorated his face every morning with ochre applied using a little matchstick. It looked magnificent. Nowadays it seems they just colour their long hair, and that in turn spreads to their backs. We wander around a bit longer but I'm not sure which is the bigger attraction: us, the rare white visitors, or the gaudily attired Samburu. I'm glad Napirai's had the chance to see a traditional market like this because they might not still be around in a few years' time.

Napirai writes: Before we set out for the market my father invites into his shop. It's quite small and there isn't much in the way of furniture but he has got a few things on offer. There are some items of clothing hanging on the wall, and a few more folded up on the ground. He points at the things hanging on the wall and asks me which I prefer. He takes down a white jacket, which is far too big for me, and puts it on me. He asks if I like it, and I nod. But then I spot a pretty black skirt hanging on the

wall and point to it. He laughs and asks if I'd prefer the skirt to the jacket. I nod, relieved to be able to swap. He's happy that he has something he can give me, and I'm really happy to get a present from him.

I put the skirt on straight away, before we head out to the market, and show my new acquisition to my mother who seems to be as delighted by it as I am. It takes us a while to get to the market. One of my legs has gone to sleep because Diego was asleep on my lap the whole time and I didn't want to wake him. I can't believe the kids here can sleep travelling over such bumpy roads.

The market place is big and I'm not sure where to start. Everything is very colourful and it's the first time I've seen so many women and men in traditional dress. It's something very out of the ordinary for me. Albert and Klaus are really excited and are dashing around trying to see everything. I go over to James's stand and sit in the shade for a while with the little children. I can see it all just as well from here.

Eventually my mother comes over to fetch me, telling me there are some women I absolutely have to meet. I notice everybody looking at us behind our backs and whispering to themselves. I'm really glad I put the skirt on because there isn't a single woman here in jeans or trousers.

The women are very pleased to meet us and stand there staring at us, but we can't talk together so the meeting doesn't last very long. I go back to play with the children again. I'm glad they came. I had to ask James specially as normally they stay at home.

The market is really enjoyable and I'm sure it makes a nice change for the locals to come here. Just sitting here watching all that's going on makes my home in Switzerland suddenly seem a long way away.

After a while we begin to get hungry and James takes us to one of the huts where they serve food, indicated by the empty teacups hanging between the cactus leaves outside. They have huge tin pots on a fire, one with rice in it, another with meat, and a third with vegetables and potatoes. We load up a plate and sit down at a cobbled-together bench inside this little cactus-built restaurant. Normally people use their right hands to eat but they fetch spoons for us. It's very tasty. A few locals come in, but disappear again as soon as they lay eyes on us.

On the way back to Stefania's stall, Lketinga introduces me to his former father-in-law. The old man doesn't miss the opportunity to get a few shillings from his son-in-law.

It seems Stefania is doing good business. There is a crowd of young, colourfully decked-out warriors standing around, being photographed by Klaus and admiring their own images on the digital display. Nobody here is exactly stressed out or in a rush. Napirai is sitting playing with Lodunu and Diego on the floor of the hut and just throws the occasional glance in the direction of these exotic warriors. The two little ones are singing Samburu songs for her. I'm very moved to see how well the two of them get on with their half-sister and cousin. I could sit here for hours, watching them and taking photographs. But I have to be careful taking pictures here because I can tell not everybody is that keen on it.

Eventually a few of the shoppers start to wander off, the warriors striding out boldly for home, their plastic bags in their hands. The women load up their donkeys who've been standing in the shade of the acacias, or wait by the sides of the cars they're hoping will give them a lift. We pack our things up too and happily head for home. For us all it was a real treat to have been at a market like this, but particularly for my companions.

There's a surprise for me when we get back: Saguna has arrived. She's sitting waiting for us with her two little children outside James's house. I'm really pleased to see her, not least because James had hinted that it would be unlikely on this visit, as she's married, has children and lives a long way away. But here she is! How wonderful! She must be in her mid-twenties by now. The last time I was here everyone was still just talking about marrying her off. I had begged for her to be spared the usual female genital mutilation. But it hadn't done any good. She looks quite a bit older now and not exactly happy. There is a sad expression about her face. But she seems happy enough when I sit down next to her and we try, with James's help, to have a conversation. She's very curious and interested to see Napirai. Saguna was only three or four years old when we left Kenya. She lived with Mama in the hut and was very close to me. She couldn't believe it when we moved from Barsaloi to Mombasa and was ill for weeks after we left.

Now here we all are sitting surrounded by children, outside James's house, telling one another stories about the old days. Then Saguna takes me the by arm and looks in envy at the red bead bracelet I bought in Nairobi. I take it off and put it on her arm as a present. She smiles for the first time.

I haven't seen Mama today so a little bit later I head over to her hut. From quite some distance I see her outside lying down on a cow skin. I'm about to turn round, not wanting to disturb her, when Saruni, James's oldest daughter, runs past me and calls out, 'Gogo, the mungu is coming!' Immediately Mama sits up and calls out, 'Suba, Corinne, serian?' I sit down next to her and we do our level best to talk to one another. She asks where the others are and I point to James's house. Before long we hear the sound of the goats coming home. The children dash past to help with the milking or just play with them. I sit there with Mama watching it all. In the distance I spot Napirai trying to have a chat with Saguna, both of them laughing away.

A bit later James comes along and asks if I have time to have a chat with the priest. We walk over to the mission. Sitting under the tree where Lketinga welcomed me on my last visit are three of the village elders. They greet me with the usual 'Supa Mama Napirai', spit in token blessing on their hands and shake mine. Then there's a torrent of talk, not one word of which I understand. But then I hear the name 'Napirai' and I begin to be a bit more careful about throwing in an automatic 'yes', and instead ask James exactly what it is they're saying. He translates, 'They're asking which of them you want to give your daughter to as a wife.' I can feel the blood drain from my face and with my heart pounding I reply, 'Apana, – none of them, no way,' shaking my head very definitely. Then one of them gives me a fixed stare in the eye and says, 'But you know we have a right to your daughter? She is a Samburu child and belongs to us.'

I turn to James looking for help and explain that this is my only daughter and she has grown up in a completely different world and cannot stay here. A few anxious moments pass while James translates what I said, and I try to stay calm. Out here the old men are the law and take all the most important decisions. They chat among themselves for a few minutes and then laugh and say, 'Okay, Corinne, we understand. But please don't forget us back here in Barsaloi. We don't have a lot and we need our children to go to school to secure a better future. Never forget that! When are you leaving?'

I tell them that unfortunately we have to go the next day, because Napirai has to be back at work in Switzerland. Then they smile and say, 'Well, you can't go without our blessing, that would be dangerous. We'll come round to James's house tomorrow at 11 a.m. and give the blessing, so you can start your journey well.' I thank them, relieved at the outcome, and hurry off to the mission with James. I shan't tell Napirai about this until we reach Nairobi, I tell myself.

The priest shows me which families get aid from charity money. It's all written down with names and amounts down to the last euro. Obviously they hope we'll continue to contribute. I make a contribution and promise that we'll continue to support them, and then we head back to the corral for our last family meal together, which Stefania has been cooking. Later that evening we all sit under the stars outside the mission, regretting that it is time for us to leave. Lketinga sits there in silence looking from me to Napirai. I would love to know what's going on in his head but his dark face, almost invisible in the dark, gives no secrets away.

More and more people come over to the mission and form a big semi-circle outside the door. I ask Lketinga what's going on, but he just shakes his head and makes some incomprehensible gesture with his hands and says, 'Corinne, I don't know why people like this.' And then I remember that they must still project films on the wall of the mission building. Around 10 p.m. James and Lketinga get up and leave. Napirai went to bed a couple of hours earlier so there is just Albert, Klaus, the driver and me left. As it's our last evening we decide we deserve a good gin and tonic, and before long we're all sitting there lost in our own thoughts. All that's running through my head is how long will it be before I'm back again, and then tiredness wins me over and I head for bed.

The next day we don't have much time as we're going to have to detour via Maralal to reach Wamba. The Wamba River has burst its banks and is impassable. Lots of people have had cars washed away by it. But I really want to show my daughter the place where she was born and take her round the little hospital where I fought for my life against malaria. But instead of three hours, the journey there is likely to take six.

We have just a little time before the elders turn up to give us their blessing, so James takes us to where my little shop used to be, though it has long since fallen down. Then he takes Napirai and me to meet one of his friends who lives in the blockhouse we lived in just behind where the shop used to be. I recognise Steven straight away. He's one of the schoolboys I used to bring home from school in Maralal for the holidays. He's only too happy to show us his house, which used to be mine. It strikes me as funny. More than twenty years ago I used to play cards here with him when he was a fifteen-year-old on his school holidays. Back then he was my guest in this house; now I'm his. Not much has changed apart from the decor. They still cook on a charcoal stove on the floor in the living room and the bedroom is still separated by just a curtain.

We don't have much time though and after looking round we go to see the third of the old school chums. Charles now works in the building trade. He's beaming all over his face as he shakes my hand and stares in amazement at Napirai. He can hardly believe how big she's grown, and fetches out an old photograph of him with baby Napirai when he came to visit us at Wamba hospital. I'm surprised because I don't even recognise the photograph. But he remembers the occasion perfectly. We chat about the good old days and I'm pleased to see that some of that first generation of schoolboys have done well for themselves. It wasn't something that could be taken for granted, given how few jobs there were.

We hear our cars starting up down at the mission. That means it's nearly time to go. We must go and see Mama again before we get our blessing for departure. We head down to her hut, still followed by a train of children. She's sitting outside waiting for us. As always she has one leg straight out in front of her, the other bent towards her, the typical sitting position for Samburu women. I sit down next to her and James translates for us. Smiling, but serious at the same time, she thanks us for coming and declares: 'I thank God, Enkai, that he has let me grow old enough to see my granddaughter Napirai again. I thank Enkai for giving me back sight in one eye so that I might look on Corinne and Napirai and recognise them. I thank Enkai for giving Corinne the strength to come back here to see us again.' As she is talking, Lketinga slowly slips away. His sister is sitting on the ground a little bit away from us, looking sad again. Saguna is peering round the corner, listening.

I have a heavy heart, though not as heavy as after my first return visit. I'm happy that Mama and Napirai had a chance to meet. I even hope that they might be able to meet again.

I would love to come back in two years when they celebrate the great traditional 'Feast of the Warriors'. It only takes place every twelve to fifteen years. They take great care in choosing a venue and spend a week singing and dancing, slaughtering lots of cows and performing all sorts of rituals. The traditional warriors cut off their long hair and divest themselves of virtually all their normal trinkets and decorations. It is a festival of great emotional importance because it marks the end of the most important part of a Samburu man's life. It marks the end of his life as a warrior, renounces all the pride and vanity that goes with the role and relinquishes his special status in society. From now on he will be seen as a 'young elder', and will be allowed to marry and start a family.

I would love to attend the festival with my daughter and if God is good, maybe Mama will still be with us. When James suggests this, she laughs and says, 'E na – of course I will.'

I joke that maybe I should take Lodunu and Diego with us as they get on so well with Napirai, but she doesn't go for that idea at all, shaking her head decisively. Everybody laughs. I thank her warmly in return and shower her with compliments. She is an amazing woman and has set a hugely important example for me. I would love to be as content with my life at her age as she is.

We put our arms around one another and hug for the last time, or try to as well as we can, given that she can't stand up. I breathe in deeply to soak up that aroma to remember her by. Then she puts her arms round Napirai too and blesses her, before Albert and Klaus come to say their goodbyes with a simple handshake. Finally we go over to James's house. I look back and see Mama drawing one open hand over her face, which is what she always does when she is trying not to show her emotions. I find it a sad sight.

In the meantime, the fifteen leading elders of the village have gathered outside James's house. Papa Saguna is one of them. Their faces are all old and lined. Each of them has some form of headgear on, either a woolly cap or a proper hat, intended as a mark of age, and they all have the same red-orange striped blanket over their shoulders.

James explains to us the ritual about to take place. 'All these men were born in Barsaloi and all of them remember you, Corinne, from the old days. Only the youngest of them speaks any English, so he is going to be their spokesman and perform the blessing. Then you must depart immediately, because they have to continue praying until you are gone.'

The English-speaking elder stands there in front of Napirai and me and says, 'Once again we warmly welcome you, Corinne, our daughter Napirai and your companions. We are very happy that you have come back to see us. We now know that you never really left us and that we remain in your thoughts. We hope that in the future too we will be always in your thoughts. You have already done much for us and when God allows, you and your friends will continue to help us here in this little patch of earth. America has its Obama, but we have our own Obama in Switzerland.'

He points to Napirai and directs his speech at her. 'Napirai, our child, we hope that you will one day come back to us again and visit your relatives. Since the day you were born you have been a part of us. We have all trusted in God that one day we would meet again. And so it has come to pass. Here we all dream that one day we will have a high school named after you. That will not be easy to achieve but it is not impossible. We can wait five or ten years if we have to. One day the children here in Barsaloi will attend Napirai High School. We thank you all and our friends in Europe who have supported us.'

And with that he takes his place again among the others. I find myself so moved that I come up with a little spontaneous speech of my own. 'Thank you all for your hospitality here in Barsaloi, now as so many years ago. I will never forget this little patch of earth; the years I spent here were the most valuable in my life even though, as a mzungu, it wasn't always easy for me, as I am sure many of you recall. I am still grateful to Lketinga that he dared take up with a white woman and to you for giving your permission. Our daughter Napirai is the result of that, and symbolises a bridge between black and white. I will continue to support Barsaloi as best I can, and perhaps together we can make your dream a reality. Than you all very much, and may God preserve you!'

James translates my words, which everybody has listened to carefully. Then they all nod or clap. Now we have to stand in front of the elders, facing west. Albert, Napirai and I stand, with our backs to them, as they begin the blessing ritual. First of all is Papa Saguna, speaking in his strong voice a few short but passionate sentences. At the end of each they all respond, 'Enkai!' and wave their sticks in the air, which is their way of reinforcing his words. It comes across as a prayer and I feel myself almost slipping into a trance, although my lips automatically form the word 'Enkai' along with them. Napirai is standing next to me, not at all sure what to make of the whole thing. This is the first time she has undergone this ceremony. Eventually Papa Saguna stops speaking and all of them spit in their hands. I look round and spot Lketinga and his wife standing a little way back, both of them praying too. Then another of the elders starts speaking and the whole thing repeats itself.

Eventually it is time to go. We are not allowed to turn round and have to leave the corral immediately while the elders all hunker down repeating their blessing over and over again, faster and faster. They will keep on like that until our vehicles have left Barsaloi. I walk straight to the car like someone hypnotised and embrace the old women waiting for us. Stefania, James and the children are there too. Lketinga leaves his wife and children and comes over to the car and, with a stiff but serious expression, hugs first Napirai and then me.

Napirai writes; I always knew that we wouldn't be here for ever but I honestly didn't expect it all to go so fast. The day of our departure has come far too soon.

My mother tells me, 'The old men want to give us a blessing before we leave'. I'm not really sure what she means by that, and as soon as they start, I'm really interested to know just what's going to happen. One of the men starts speaking and it goes on and on until they've all done the same. I find it very moving that they all need to say so many prayers for our journey. The whole ritual is amazing and quite unlike anything I've ever experienced. After the blessing comes the hard part, which I've not been looking forward to at all: saying goodbye to everybody. I start with James and his wife, hugging them hard and thanking them for the good time they've shown us. It's sad saying goodbye but it's not a sad occasion: I'm really pleased that James tells me to come back any time and that they will think of my mother and me and pray for us. It's really great to hear him say that and I'm very touched. Then we say goodbye to the rest of the family and the other people of the village. I shake hand after hand, but at least this time I know most of them, although that only makes saying goodbye harder.

I can't say goodbye individually to all the children; there are far too many of them. So I just wave to all of them. I've grown really close to the children in our family and find it hard to leave them. It almost breaks my heart to say farewell to my little half-brother Lodunu. I wish I could take them all with me.

The little ones are very sad to see us go and don't really understand what's happening, Diego in particular. When he sees we're about to leave, he starts crying and holds on tight to my leg. It takes Stefania to come and prise him off.

As we're finally about to leave I look around for my father, Lketinga, and see him sitting on a wall watching it all. When he spots me looking at him, he comes over and hugs me, gives me a kiss on the cheek and tells me to look after myself and come back soon. Saying goodbye like this is hard for both of us.

Then we get into the car and slowly set off. I wave and wave until they've all vanished from sight, and the tears are rolling down my cheeks.

I climb into the car, with the voices of the elders still in my ears. I wave goodbye again to Lketinga and he nods to me and replies in a rough voice, 'Ayia!'

It's very quiet in the car, Napirai and I both sunk in our own thoughts. Of course, I am sad that it's all over but on the other hand I'm pleased everything went so well and that the elders gave us such a powerful and dramatic farewell blessing. That means a lot to the locals and it's important for us too. For a long time I sense I can still feel its effect.

From now on my daughter can make up her own mind if and when she wants to go and see her African family. I am quite certain that in time she will be able to understand how important this visit was. And I am equally certain that she will come back again.

Shankayon is sitting in the back with Napirai, but doesn't say a word during the whole journey to Maralal. She had to get out there because we are heading on to Wamba. But when Martin, the driver, asks where we should let her out, she doesn't reply. Martin turns and looks at us and says, 'I think she'd rather go with you.'

The next few minutes are heartbreaking. It's quite clear Shankayon doesn't want to be separated from Napirai. Tears run silently down her cheeks as she reluctantly gets out of the car. I get out with her, give her a big hug and the money for her bus fare so that at least she doesn't have to walk all the way home to her mother. But even as we set off again Shankayon's sadness travels a long way with us.

The trip to Wamba is long and the road dry and dusty, but eventually, late in the afternoon, we reach the hospital. The doors are locked, however, and I have to explain to the confused doorman that my daughter was born here, and all I want to do is show her round. At first he doesn't believe me, but then he makes a telephone call and I have to tell somebody else the same thing, and at last we're allowed in.

The hospital isn't as busy as it used to be. It doesn't take me long to find the maternity department and even the room I shared with Sophia. Everything looks just as it did twenty-one years ago. Even the bedclothes, the iron bed frame and the metal cupboards where the cockroaches used to make their nests if I stored anything edible inside, are all still there, as if time had stood still.

Napirai owes her life, and I owe my survival, to the doctors and nurses in this hospital. On several occasions it was their last-minute intervention that saved my life. Despite the fact that compared with our modern hospitals everything here was – and still is – a lot more basic, here at the end of the world it was the difference between life and death.

Napirai writes: Saying goodbye to Shankayon is really hard. But I'm looking forward to seeing where I was born. It's a bit of a detour but I really want to see Wamba hospital and can't wait to know if anything has changed. I've seen my mother's photos of it so often.

The first things I notice when we arrive are the pretty red shrubs with lots of flowers that I was always amazed by on the photos. I'm astonished they're still here.

The hospital is very basic. I thought that by now it might have got a bit more modern but it seems very little has changed. It all looks a bit moribund to me. But I'm glad to be here and somehow or other the place has a strangely calming influence on me. I ask my mother to take a few photos of me alongside the shrubs to remember it by.

We wander round for a bit and even find a room where there are some newborn babies, on the other side of a protective

glass window. Once upon a time, I was one of those. I smile to
myself.

After our tour we get back into the car and set off towards the Samburu lodge where we intend to spend the night. The lodge is in a national park, and on the way there we spot a family of elephants and herds of zebra and buffalo. After we book into our excellent room, we take a walk about and pop into the souvenir shop. Among the various literature about Kenya, I come across three copies of my own book in the English translation.

It amazes me that wherever I go in Africa I find the English translation of my books, not just in Nairobi, but out here in the bush. It makes me terribly proud. Just for the sake of it, I buy two copies of *The White Masai* to give to our drivers. The girl at the cash desk is astonished that I'm buying two copies of the same book, and asks me if I know it's a true story. I laugh and tell her, 'Yes, I know, it's my story', and point at the photo of the author. She can hardly believe it.

By evening the word has got around. The staff start looking at Napirai and me differently. The next day, just as we are about to set off, a Jeep roars up and three armed policemen jump out, followed by a very large gentleman. I think nothing of it and just stand there with our driver waiting for Albert and Klaus. Several minutes go by during which one of the policemen has a chat with our driver. I understand none of it, and then Martin asks me if he might introduce the police chief for northern Kenya. He wants me to sign a copy of *The White Masai* for him and be photographed alongside him. I'm bemused. Somehow word of our presence has got to the big boss along the bush telegraph from a region where there isn't even mobile phone reception. It's a new experience for me to have an important police official ask me to sign a book for him. Before he and his men set off he makes a point of telling us that there are no problems along the road to Nairobi, and wishes us bon voyage.

It's still a long road though, driving through the desert dust until eventually, unexpectedly, we come across a broad highway. It seems the Chinese are building new roads everywhere in Kenya. This is the first in the Samburu region and hard by the side of the new asphalt surface stand a few manyattas. But it's dangerous for people or animals to live this close to a road where instead of 20kph cars rush past at closer to 80kph. The locals can't judge distance and speeds like that, at least not properly, and there are apparently regular accidents. But they are still proud of their new road, which has brought civilisation closer.

Hours later we finally reach Nairobi and traffic chaos of a completely different sort. Martin slowly battles through the jams to the Fairview Hotel, where we are to spend the last night before Napirai and Albert leave for home.

I would have liked to spend a few days with Napirai talking over the whole experience but I realise she has to come to terms with it on her own. She is twenty years old and has just met her father for the first time, as well as her grandmother and the entire African side of her family. For the first time in nearly two decades she is back on African soil and has experienced a part of the culture she comes from, rather than just seeing it on television. And all of that in a short space of time, broken up by long journeys, is both physically and psychologically taxing. Right now she needs some time to take it in and come to terms with it.

Napirai writes; I've been looking forward to this journey for so long and now it's all over. Not so long ago I wouldn't have believed it was possible. For ages I wasn't even sure I wanted to come to Kenya. I was always just a little afraid of the unknown. But in the end my own growing interest in it all, backed up

by encouragement from people who mean a lot to me, gave me the courage to make the trip, and today I am proud and pleased to have done so.

I'm really happy that I have such a warm family. The visit exceeded all my expectations. Meeting my father was one of the most important moments in my life, and I am so grateful for it.

I don't know what will happen in the future but I know that this trip has given me strength. And I know what loving people I have to rely on.

I've been enchanted by this little part of Africa that I've seen and one day I shall definitely return.

A BIG SURPRISE IN MOMBASA

After my daughter reluctantly takes her leave, Klaus and I have a week of intensive work to do back here in Nairobi. I want to go back and see the slum-dwellers with their 'Gardens in a Sack', as well as the Jamii Bora women, just to find out how they've all got on in the five months since I last saw them. After that we're going to fly down to Mombasa where I hope to find Priscilla. I've never been able to forgive myself for not getting back in touch with the woman to whom I owe so much. On the last trip to Kenya I couldn't get in touch with her. But this time I'm determined to make sure I do. I devote an entire week to finding her. I would really like to meet up with her again, and tie up that loose end.

It is only a short flight from Nairobi to Mombasa, but immediately the atmosphere is different. The air is sultry and tastes of the sea. It's a tropical air and it immediately makes me think I've come on my holidays. I remember being taken with it the first time I landed here, twenty-four years ago. But Klaus and I soon discover that in the meantime Mombasa has been stuck in perpetual traffic jams. It takes for ever sitting in a jam of cars before we reach Tamarind Village in the city centre. This is a nice hotel complex with a restaurant terrace from where there is a beautiful view over the old harbour.

Over dinner a gentle breeze from the sea that comes in round the picturesque curved terrace gives everything an almost oriental feel. The harbour lights are reflected in the sea.

It would be a wonderful setting for a romantic evening or, in my case, for a chance to reflect on my life story. First thing tomorrow I am going down to the south coast to feel the white sand of Diani Beach beneath my feet. Down there I hope to be able to find some link to Priscilla, even though I know that without any leads it isn't going to be easy, and might even be impossible.

Priscilla is a Masai woman with whom I lived for several months when I came to Kenya but initially couldn't find Lketinga again. She helped me through those hard days. I lived with her in a modest little roundhouse set back a little from Diani Beach. She helped me in any way she could. She even took me on a long journey to see her family in the Narok highlands. That was an experience I'll never forget. At night it was as cold as it is in the Swiss mountains in autumn. In the mornings there was a mist and dew on the trees and grass. I had to put on every bit of clothing I had before going to bed at night, and even still nearly froze to death in the simple little hut I stayed in. And then there were the little creatures – fleas or something – that crawled all over me at night. I hardly slept a wink all week, and even when we thankfully got back to Mombasa I still had lice.

But Priscilla was my best African female friend and I was proud of the fact that she had invited me to go with her to her home and meet her mother, who looked after her four children while she worked in Mombasa to earn money. Her family had never had a white guest before and so they showered Masai jewellery on me, and piled roast goat meat in front of me.

Even years later, when Lketinga and I with baby Napirai left Barsaloi and came to Mombasa, Priscilla let us stay in her tiny living room in Kamau village until we found a room of our own. She tried to help us all she could, even when things were difficult with Lketinga and he got jealous even of her and wouldn't let me see her.

The next day we hire a car and set out slowly through the stop–go traffic to the Likoni ferry, which we need to take to cross the sea inlet to the south coast. There is now a three-lane queue for the ferry. When I first used it there were very few cars and it was easy to drive straight on, even though the ferry itself was smaller. I sit there in the car, people-watching. The passengers haven't changed much. There are thousands of them standing on the quayside waiting for the cars to load so they too can board. Many of them, particularly the women, are carrying huge burdens on their heads, some of them wooden crates crammed full of chickens, other have sacks of vegetables that are obviously very heavy. In among them are home-made hand carts, each of which several young men struggle to manage. They are clearly used to it, but still find it hard work, with sweat rolling down their foreheads and the veins bulging on their muscular arms. These people don't need to go to the gym, I think to myself.

Meanwhile people keep knocking on the car windows, trying to sell things to us. One has a few strings of beads, a child is selling sweets and roasted nuts. It's hard to say no to all of them.

Eventually we board the massive ferry. It's a déjà vu experience for me. This is where I first saw Lketinga back in 1986 and my life's love story began. Up until then I would never have imagined that from that moment on the entire direction of my life would change and that today my story would be read all over the world. Even today I get letters from tourists who have used the ferry to get to hotels on the south coast, which say things like: 'Dear Corinne, it was a really strange feeling to stand on that ferry. The whole time I could think of nothing but your incredible love story…'

The foot passengers are all crowded on to the upper deck, but some even stand between the cars. I'm astonished when I realise that this new ferry was built in Germany, in Laube-gast. My readers in the former East Germany will be delighted to know that the famous ferryboats built in their part of the country now carry up to 170,000 people a day here, along with several thousand vehicles.

Eventually we near the other side, where there are huge posters with pictures of Nelson Mandela, Mother Teresa, Martin Luther King and Mama Caro. But it's hard to say whether they're adverts for UNICEF or the Imperial Bank. Then the ferry ramp drops with a resounding crash and gradually the cars start up and drive off. We make a point of driving carefully because already people have pushed past us.

Not much on this side of the inlet has changed. There are still shacks close together along the roadside where people work or sell things. There are women covered in black chadors grilling sweetcorn on little charcoal stoves. Like everywhere else there are pedlars wandering around trying to sell souvenirs or other knick-knacks to us while the car is still trundling along at walking pace. Eventually we reach a relatively modern road leading towards Ukunda. Everything is very green at the moment and there are tall palms growing between the little wooden huts along the shore. A few goats are tied to the trees on long leads that allow them room to roam and graze.

Shortly before we reach Ukunda it starts raining so heavily that visibility is reduced to a minimum. Before long the pools of water by the side of the road have turned into lakes and I start to give up hope of finding Priscilla today. I don't even know where to start. My original idea was to visit the hotels I know along the beach and ask some of the kanga-sellers if they knew her. But with rain like this that's not going to be any good as both the tourists and the pedlars will all have deserted the beaches.

We stop at a simple little tearoom to watch the people go by. A few elderly men in white kaftans and white headdresses are sitting at a table watching a television hung from the wall, which is showing some big parade in Nairobi. At another table are two young couples, apparently Englishmen doting on new Kenyan girlfriends. I smile to myself, wondering how these love stories will pan out.

After a couple of hours the rain dies down and we set off again to the mission in Ukunda to visit a famous missionary there. He doesn't recognise me immediately, but when I tell him I'm the 'White Masai' he catches on and invites us in for tea. He tells Klaus, to his astonishment, that he turned up in his Land Rover in Barsaloi by chance on his way to visit Father Giuliani on the very day I was getting married in my white European wedding dress. Giuliani told him what was happening and he could hardly believe that a young white woman had voluntarily decamped to the wilderness of Barsaloi. I can still hear the amazement in his voice as he recounts what he considered to be an extraordinary decision to take. Before we leave he shows us round his little school. Every class we enter has the children leaping to their feet to sing songs for us.

We drive back to Mombasa and hope the weather will be better tomorrow. Yet again we have to queue in a traffic jam for an hour to catch the ferry. On the other side Klaus manages to negotiate our way through the traffic chaos, which I'm grateful for because I wouldn't trust myself to manage it. Under the circumstances it seems even more incredible that twenty years ago even Lketinga managed to drive around here.

The weather the next day is no better, however, so we decide to postpone things again rather than go through the same difficult journey down the coast. Instead we spend our time wandering around Mombasa's old city centre. We park next to the famous Fort Jesus by the old harbour. I wander down the narrow little lanes where the oriental atmosphere is most concentrated. The houses are narrow and tall with twisting balconies and long flights of steps. Most of them are painted white and have heavy wooden doors either decorated with metal or elaborately carved. At first I come across mainly tourist shops with remarkable wooden masks and carvings, but as soon as I turn into a little alleyway, I'm in another world. Here the old, crumbling houses are covered with washing hung out to dry. Women are wandering around in their chadors or sitting on the bare earth together chatting. Some of the alleyways are so small that you could lean out of one door and shake hands with your neighbour across the street. There are pots steaming away on charcoal stoves outside most of the doors. Every bit of flat wall space is used, either to display vegetables for sale, or to take a little nap on. In one backyard I spot a little Muslim girl looking after a turkey poking around in the dust. Everything here in the back streets is a lot more relaxed and laid back than the hectic chaos of the main market streets I eventually find myself back in.

Here there are big crowds of people and I get shoved along so fast that there's hardly time to look at all the wares spread out on the ground. Some people are selling fish or vegetables, other plastic plates and cutlery. The main market hall smells of meat, fish and spices. Here and there are sacks filled to overflowing with yellow or red spice powders. Everybody is fighting for attention, trying to sell their goods. Hustlers try to drag me over to one stall or another in the hope of getting a tip from the merchant. Before long I wish I was back in the calm of the backstreet. I push past sacks of rice and beans to make my way along the street to find the way back to the fort. But all of a sudden I find myself in another calm little alleyway, standing in amazement in front of a narrow blue-painted building covered with iron bars, with just a little sign saying 'Jewellery'. Obviously there are valuables inside. Next to it are three men sitting in the shade making leather sandals.

An elaborately carved door decorated with brass opens and a horde of school children pile out, the boys in their long white kaftans with little white skull caps, the girls with white headdresses and long tunics. The modern schoolbags on their backs seem somehow an anachronism.

I pass the large white-painted mosque and end up on the square by Fort Jesus. There are lots of little fishing boats bobbing in the water and it feels as if I've stumbled on to some scene from long ago. Everything here is totally different from increasingly modern Nairobi.

Next morning, thankfully, the sun comes out. In fact it is one of those picture postcard days when Mombasa's coast looks like it does in holiday brochures. We set out immediately after breakfast but it still takes us two hours to get to the south coast. When we get past Ukunda I start looking for the retail complex where Lketinga and I had our souvenir shop. But when we find the building, which is now showing its age, there are no longer any shops in it. The whole building has been turned into apartments. It has a much bigger effect on me than it did six years ago. This is where we tried to make a new start. The shop was doing well and everything had been just great until Lketinga became consumed with jealousy and flipped out.

I was pleased to discover on our visit to Barsaloi that he has changed dramatically in this respect. He is extremely loving and has a lot of respect for his third wife and their children. There was no sign of him torturing her with his jealousy. Quite on the contrary. In fact she seemed relatively happy and very self-confident. And he himself seemed very content and at peace with the world, a respected village elder. I was relieved to see that.

I drag myself away from those painful memories and we head off again, past several supermarkets, although I am happy to see that the little native shops along the beach are back. More than twenty years ago, when the first supermarket opened, they were all torn down. Obviously people have since realised that competition is good and that lots of tourists would rather see the native artists and watch them at work.

We are now getting closer to the area I still call 'mine'. As we pass the Africana Sea Lodge, I tell Klaus, 'Slow down, please. I want to remember it all the way it used to be. I have a gut feeling that we can't be too far from Kamau village, which was my last home here before returning to Switzerland. Priscilla was my neighbour here.'

There's excitement in my voice and Klaus turns to me expectantly and says, 'So where exactly is it then?'

All I can do is shrug my shoulders and say, 'Somewhere around here, there's a track that leads into the bush, but I can't be sure which because there used to be just one and now there are lots. But we just have to pick one at random and then ask people.'

Klaus isn't exactly impressed by this but he agrees to give it a go. Our hire car isn't exactly designed for tracks like this either. But there's no way I'm going to be deflected from following my intuition.

Just like in the old days, there are baboons all over the place, but now there are lots of new buildings in between the old-style shacks. In fact, it has all changed so much that my memory is little help. We stop by the side of the street and I ask some men standing there, 'Do you know where is Kamau village?' But they just repeat 'Kamau village' to one another and shake their heads. We stop and ask a hotel concierge but get no more joy. That leaves us no option but to try something different.

The first track we take leads us to a luxurious villa hurriedly thrown up behind a barbed wire fence. A few locals watch suspiciously as Klaus tries to do a U-turn. But I'm not going to give up so easily. I'm determined to find my old friend Priscilla, if she's still here to be found. We drive back to the asphalt road, go on a few hundred metres and then take the next turning into the bush. We spot a couple standing outside a little shop and stop while I ask them if they know Kamau village. They answer with silence and shaking heads. But somehow or other I have the feeling this is the right way. Then a woman in a coloured headdress standing behind two newly slaughtered goats hanging from hooks calls out to me, 'Go ahead and later left side,' waving a huge knife in the air to indicate the direction she means.

I give Klaus a big smile and ask him to drive on. He looks at me sceptically but I no longer have any doubt. We bump along over ruts and clumps of grass and just as we reach a cross-roads, beyond which the bush is thicker than ever, we meet a woman coming towards us with a water canister on her head. I ask her if she knows Kamau village and she tells us to keep going until we reach a stone wall, and the entrance is just past it. But that only makes me doubt we're on the right track as there certainly didn't used to be a stone wall. When we reach it Klaus drives along its length slowly, and then all of a sudden we find ourselves in the middle of Kamau village.

The settlement is bigger than it used to be. My eyes are drawn to a big tree in the middle with lots of lads sitting chatting around it, who immediately start staring at us. But just behind them I spot my former home. I'm overcome by emotion and call out, 'Klaus, look, Napirai and I used to live on the other side of that tin door. She used to climb up this tree. I could cry with joy.'

I leap out of the car and can hear Klaus behind me calling out, 'Be careful, Corinne.' But I pay no heed. It feels as if I've come home, for 'home' was what this little hut used to be for seven months, my last refuge before I fled Kenya. I left behind everything but the clothes on my back on the other side of this tin door: all my photos, all my personal stuff, even my white wedding dress.

I walk up to the doubtful-looking lads around the tree and ask them if they know a Masai woman called Priscilla who sells kangas on the beach. I can hardly believe their answer: 'Yes, we know her!' How can I possibly have found her so easily? One of the lads jumps up and runs ahead of me, but stops at a door and says, 'This house belongs to the lady you are looking for.' The door is open. Klaus has parked the car and is busy trying to keep the assembled horde of kids away from it, as well as stopping them from tugging on his trouser legs. He's really not happy at all.

I stand by the door and shout aloud, 'Hello!' Immediately two girls appear, each holding a child by the hand. I ask them if they know Priscilla and they nod, but they speak little English.

They gesture to me to come in and sit down on one of the sofas. I sit down, realising that they have sent word to Priscilla but that it might take some time. Klaus is waiting outside with the car, so I take in the room in a bit more detail. Clearly things have got better for my old friend. Her house has at least two or three rooms, though clearly several people live here. There's a mobile phone on the table in front of the sofa and there's even a little fridge in the corner. That means they must have electricity now. There are a few paintings, calendars and some Masai art hanging on the walls.

I sit there waiting, trying to talk to the girls while the whole time tiny children try to climb into my lap. But after waiting some time with no sign of Priscilla, and spending most of it looking round the room, it dawns on me that this just doesn't look like her sort of place. I ask them if they have a photo of her. One of the girls disappears and comes back with a photo, but one glance at it makes me realise that this is clearly a different Priscilla. The woman in the photo is obviously a Masai, but a lot younger and slimmer than the Masai woman I'm looking for. Disappointed, I hand the photo back to them and explain there's been a misunderstanding.

We're just about to set off when the little girl runs out with the mobile, talking into it all the while. All I can make out is that she's telling somebody there's two white people here looking for a Priscilla. I give her my name and she passes it on. There follows a bit of an interchange, then suddenly she hands me the phone. 'Hello?' I say, and immediately from the other end comes a torrent of laughter and talk. 'Corinne, it's me. Eddy. I can't believe you're in my house. Stay where you are, Corinne, I'll be there shortly. I'm down on the beach but I'll be back as soon as I can, my friend!'

I'm totally amazed and promise to wait. By some strange miracle my search for Priscilla has led me to Eddy!

Eddy was a friend of Lketinga's when I first met him. He was the one who helped me find my way around all the jails along the coast after Lketinga was locked up for being involved in a fight. Later on he was also a real help to me in all sorts of difficult situations. And now, all of a sudden, just when I least expected it, I'm about to see him again.

Before long a dented white car drives up and Eddy leaps out. He charges over to me with such force that he nearly knocks me over, throws his arms around me and starts babbling away. There are tears in the corners of his eyes as he thanks God for bringing us together again. I recognise him straight away, even if he has aged. He still wears Masai jewellery round his neck and keeps his dyed red hair under a headscarf. He hasn't lost his mischievous look as he invites me into his house and offers me a cool cola. That's luxury out here! Then he tells me just how weird the coincidence is that I've ended up in his house. He moved here from Ukunda a couple of years ago with a Samburu woman and her three children. It just so happens that her name is also Priscilla. We both fall about laughing.

He wants to know everything, particularly about Napirai, whom he last saw when she was a tiny child. I tell him we've just been to see Lketinga, which makes him really happy. We chat about the old days, with him beaming at me. He asks after my brother and sister, both of whom he remembers, my sister in particular. He introduces me to his three daughters and proudly shows me their school reports. His only problem is paying the school fees.

After a while I ask him about 'my' Priscilla and he says, 'Yes, she's still working on the beach, selling her stuff.'

I can hardly wait to see her when he tells me this. We all set off in the car down to the beach, Eddy saying all the time how happy he is to see me again. I have to admit I'm pretty emotional too. The coast is so vast that it is almost impossible that I should have found the two people who meant so much to me twenty years ago.

We turn in next to the Robinson Hotel and park the car in a dead-end street next to the beach, where there are lots of stalls. Eddy dashes off towards the sea, only to stop by one of the stalls where he starts chatting away and waving his hands.

Within moments a plump woman in a white headdress and flowery blouse appears: unmistakably 'my' Priscilla!

She stands there staring at me, wide-eyed, throw her hands to her face and says, 'It's you, Corinne! I don't believe it! My sister!'

I rush up to her in delight and hug her. She seems overwhelmed by the surprise and has tears in her eyes. All this time there's an Italian woman waiting impatiently at her stall trying to pay. Priscilla says, 'Corinne, one minute while I deal with this customer, then I'm yours!' All the time she is packing up the goods for her customer, she is shaking her head in disbelief, repeating over and over, 'Thank you, God, for bringing my sister back to me.' Meanwhile. I'm fighting back the tears too and saying a little prayer of my own.

I can see that she is now running a really first-class souvenir stall. Eddy tells me she has another one too, selling kangas right on the beachfront. Meanwhile Priscilla deals with her remaining customers and comes over and hugs me. She tells me she has asked lots of tourists if they know me and even given them letters to send to me. But obviously none of them got to me. I tell her I've moved house frequently and finding the right address would not have been easy.

She introduces me to her two sons, who both also run stalls. She has worked hard and even been able to build a small house for herself in the Masai country, and regularly goes back there to see her grandchildren. She only came back to Mombasa a week ago as the tourist trade is just picking up again. I can't believe how lucky I've been.

Priscilla can hardly believe that I've popped up from nowhere like this. Eddy tells her how we bumped into one another. The story amuses her and she gives a broad smile, revealing the same old gap in her front teeth. She asks one of her sons to fetch us a cold drink, then asks me about Napirai. I tell her about our visit to Barsaloi and she can hardly believe it. I show her photos of the trip on my camera's screen. Obviously, she's disappointed that Napirai didn't come down here to the coast with me. But she understands the demands of education: she has brought up four children of her own.

As we have lunch together I tell her that I came back to Diani Beach six years previously and tried to find her. But it took my determination – and a lot of luck – to pull it off this time so that we can sit here together.

We share a few memories of the old days and she tells me how terribly sad she was when I left. She couldn't understand why I hadn't said anything to her, until she got the letter I sent her from Switzerland. For a moment I feel a lump in my throat.

Eddy tells us lots of tourists ask him if he's the Eddy in my book and whether he knows me. Being able to say 'yes' has done him no harm at all in helping to sell his Masai stuff. Priscilla can tell a similar story: most people now call her Mama Masai and hardly ever use her real name. But how lucky were we to end up by accident in Eddy's house; otherwise we would certainly never have found her!

We go back down to the beach, because she still has to do business. There are new tourists arriving today, Priscilla says. I take a look at what she has to offer on her stall and can't help casting my mind back to the things we had for sale in our shop. A few tourists stop to look and I find myself chatting to them, just to help her sell a few more things. Most of them are astounded to find that they've just landed and already bumped into the 'White Masai'. A lot of them had been talking about me on the plane, they say! How about that!

The next day, Sunday, we're still delighted that we've found one another again, and in the meantime, word has got around that I'm in town. Lots of Samburu warriors keep coming up from the beach, talking to me and asking about Napirai. It would seem a lot of them have heard of my girl.

Priscilla is wearing her Sunday best and has calmed down a bit. She tells me, 'I could hardly sleep all night. I kept thanking

God that he brought you back here. I kept thinking of the great adventure we had together. I could see it all as if it were yesterday, and yet in reality it was twenty years ago!'

We sit there together on a tree stump on the idyllic beach, eating wonderful tropical fruit and listening to the sound of the sea, just happy to enjoy the magical moment.

Later that afternoon Eddy takes his leave: he has to perform in a Masai dance at one of the hotels and needs to sort out things for the other participants. I promise to send him photos and find some sponsors for his gifted children's school fees. We hug and say goodbye.

When it comes time to say goodbye to Priscilla too, she gets rather melancholy and says, 'It would have been so nice if you could have stayed a bit longer, sister.' She takes a little hand-painted picture of an African round hut with a couple standing in front of it and says, 'Give this to Napirai, so maybe she might remember the time she spent with me. Tell her, that that's the way her mummy and I used to live. Tell her that if she ever comes to Mombasa, I'll always be here.'

I have to choke back a sob. We hug one another and with our final handshake I pass her some money to tide her over for a few weeks.

I say farewell to my newly rediscovered friend there on Diani Beach, where she stands quietly and modestly as I listen to the sea until finally it is time for me to climb into the car and leave my tempestuous past behind me.

After my return to Switzerland I get the following letter from Priscilla:

How are you, sister? I hope you had a good journey home.
I can still hardly believe you were here. I'm so happy we
managed to meet up again and believe God placed only a few
hills between us. I wish you could have stayed here for a year.
Please come back soon. I am intending to buy something to

keep with the money you gave me, something that will always remind me of you every time I look at it. God bless you so much. May God protect you, my dear friend.

AFTERWORD

Even though my initial plan was to shake off the 'White Masai' tag, the visit Napirai and I paid to Barsaloi made clear to me that I will never lose my links to my African family. On the contrary, they have become more important to me than ever. The warm reception and hospitality they showed us proved to me that they still consider us part of them and are endlessly grateful for all our support. The fact that Lketinga and I have a daughter together links us for life.

But it is not just the family and cultural links that tie me to Africa. The past two years have proved to me that I love this continent like my own child. If I stand on my lawn, with the grass between my toes, and let my thoughts wander where they will, it is always to my experiences in Africa that they return. That is what makes my pulse race, that is what inspires my dreams. The energy, the happiness, the sheer love of life, combined with their simple lifestyle, will always work their magic on me. Sometimes it gives me strength, but sometimes it also makes me feel small and humble.

I have come to realise how well we live back in Europe. Most people have a roof over their heads, running water, toilets, electricity, televisions, fridges, a bed and heating when they need it. We have everything we need to get us through life.

But in the eyes of Africans what makes us poor is the loneliness that comes with our 'luxury'. We have left our family and community life behind us in favour of unbridled egoism.

Loneliness thrives in our society and many people only communicate via the Internet. Our apartments keep getting bigger but the number of family members living in them shrinks. It gets easier to avoid other people, to be trapped within our own four walls.

Obviously, wealthy people in Africa also enjoy modern luxury, but they remain a tiny minority.

What a lot of Africans don't understand when they look at 'white' society is the stress we live with, the hard, serious look on our faces all the time. In their eyes, we have everything to live an easy, relaxed life. We just don't know it.

Much of what attracts me to Africa, of course, is the intangible, the immovable, the unpredictable, the chaos, the animals, the sheer wildness that is Africa's alone.

And then what would Africa be without the warm hearts, love of life and fun demonstrated by its inhabitants. Whether in east Africa or southwest Africa, it is this mixture of faith in God, love of live and laid-back attitude to life, despite the tough conditions they live under, that will forever fascinate me. They have a life that money cannot buy. We can only try to absorb a little of it, to keep it in our hearts.

For me, Africa is a passion – a lifelong love story.

Dear readers

Thank you for your interest in my new book. Given that I contribute from my income, by buying this book you have already contributed a little to my 'White Masai' Kenya foundation.

If you should be inspired to give further support to any of the projects, you can do so directly. For my part I guarantee that the money will be used well and that you will be told what it is used for.

Perhaps you too could help us build the school in Barsaloi.

Many thanks, and lots of love,

Corinne and Napirai.

THE 'WHITE MASAI' KENYA FOUNDATION

We are a charitable foundation based in Switzerland. Our main purpose is to support the health and education projects described in this book and also to provide self-help aid by cooperating with local institutions.

www.solidarites.org
www.jamiibora.org
www.mysakenya.org
Schulprojekt Barsaloi

If you would like to become a member or just want to know more please visit:
www.foerderverein-kenia-weisse-massai.ch
Förderverein Kenia WEISSE MASSAI
Lugano/Schweiz info@fwkwm.ch

Contributions from EU countries should be made via:
Förderverein Kenia WEISSE MASSAI
Account number: 20033036
Sort code: 700 202 70
UniCredit Bank AG – Hypovercinsbank
IBAN: DE14 7002 0270 0010 0220 26
BIC/SWIFT: HYVEDEMMXXX

THE FOUR-MILLION-COPY BESTSELLER

THE WHITE
MASAI

Corinne Hofmann

'What an amazing story! One of the bravest and most vivid
I've read in years, I'm not surprised it's a bestseller'
DEBORAH MOGGACH

REUNION IN
BARSALOI

FROM THE AUTHOR OF THE FOUR-MILLION COPY BESTSELLER

Corinne Hofmann

'The hit book *The White Masai*...
an extraordinary story'
Libby Purves, BBC *Midweek*

BACK FROM AFRICA

FROM THE AUTHOR OF THE
FOUR-MILLION COPY BESTSELLER
CORINNE HOFMANN

'A startling experience [with] riveting
exotica and intriguing human relationships'
The Hollywood Reporter on *The White Masai*